And They Persisted . . .

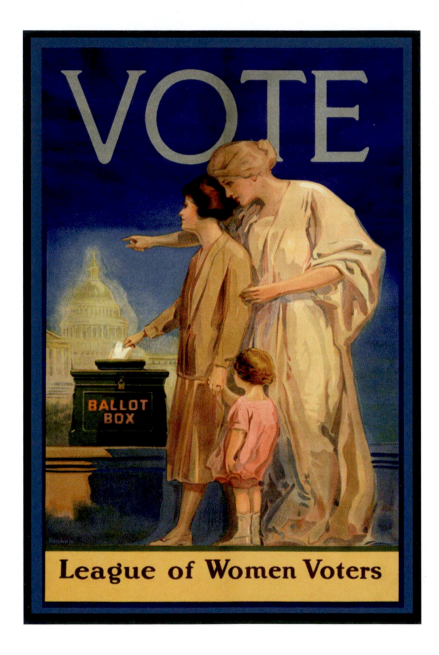

And They Persisted …

A Century of Impact by Iowa Leagues

Linda Meloy

League of Women Voters of Johnson County
Iowa City, Iowa

DEDICATION

We honor and thank the Johnson County League
members who made this book possible:

Jean Lloyd-Jones, former Iowa legislator (1979–95) and longtime
League member who served as president of the League of Women
Voters of Iowa (1971–74), for her insights, knowledge, consistent
encouragement, and determination to lift more women into
decision-making positions in government;

Pat Jensen, Life League member, a former League of Women Voters
of Iowa president (2003–05), and League of Women Voters of the US
Board member (1982–86), for her wealth of knowledge of the League
and its processes that she has shared generously, and her consistent
mentoring of novices to the League; and

Two longtime League members who provided financial support and
requested anonymity, which is the status of the hundreds of League
members across Iowa who have not received accolades for their hard
work improving government for all. They all were truly committed
to the League's principles, processes, and positions.

Jean Lloyd-Jones   Pat Jensen

Contents

Acknowledgements

COMPILING THIS centennial history of the League of Women Voters of Iowa has been a most enriching task for this longtime League member. In true League manner, though, it has taken a team to "get 'er done."

Thanks are in order to the many who have assisted with this effort: Dr. Pam Stek, research assistant; League colleague Linda Schreiber; Melissa Ballard Auen, copy editor; Sara Sauers, book designer; Robyn Hepker, Benson Hepker Design; members of the League of Women Voters of Johnson County, including Gail Zlatnik and the Century of Impact Committee; the eleven local League presidents and their members; board members of the League of Women Voters of Iowa and Karen Person, web master; interviewees—past presidents of the state League and League members who served in the Legislature; the staffs at the University of Iowa Women's Archives, the Carrie Chapman Catt Center at Iowa State University, and the Iowa State Historical Society (Des Moines and Iowa City); the "Ding" Darling Wildlife Society for permission to reprint "Ding's" cartoons, and the *Des Moines Register* for the reprinting of Frank Miller's cartoons.

And, a thank you to a large circle of old friends far and wide who listened to or read correspondence about the book, always supportive but questioning if I was crazy to take on such a responsibility! The Epilogue addresses the perception of "crazy" Leaguers, so get to reading!

Donors

The League of Women Voters of Johnson County's Century of Impact Committee recognizes the following businesses and individuals who donated to the Centennial Campaign to support LWVJC centennial projects and programming.

John Balmer
The Mary Bryant Fund
Syndy and Jim Conger
Lensing Funeral
MidWestOne Bank
Gerald and Carol Nordquist
Quality Care Storage Company
Tom Scott
Nancy and Allen Thomas
Two anonymous donors

In-kind sponsors: Every Bloomin' Thing, *The Gazette*, Iowa Book and Supply, Iowa Women's Foundation, Iowa City *Press-Citizen*, the University of Iowa Pentacrest Museums, the University of Iowa

THIS BOOK PROJECT HAS BEEN FUNDED PRIMARILY BY FOUR JOHNSON COUNTY LEAGUE MEMBERS.

Prologue

WELCOME TO an inside view of the work of countless Iowans who have been involved in the continual task of making democracy work at local and state levels of government. For one hundred years, members of the League of Women Voters of Iowa and local Leagues across the state have been doing just that—making democracy work. This "LWV Centennial Rap" by former Iowa legislator Johnie Hammond and fellow Ames & Story County League member Mim Patterson sums it up:

> We're the League of Women Voters and we're here to say
> We practice being citizens a certain way.
> Research and careful study is where it's at.
> We're thankful to our founder, Carrie Chapman Catt.
> One hundred years ago she said the vote is good
> For men and also women whom she said should
> Participate and vote and represent the nation;
> You can't have democracy with no participation!
> We study on the question, looking for the best solution.
> Then we lobby the elected folks for each proposition.
> The issues are diverse and the problems mixed.
> There are lots and lots of problems needing to be fixed.
> Like sentencing reform and juvenile detention,
> Burgeoning poverty and preschool education.
> Environmental garbage must have our close attention,
> Not to mention issues of gross discrimination.
> Every person voting is vital to our nation
> So we dedicate our time to voter registration.
> Suppression of the vote we cannot tolerate …
> We really have to stop it to have justice in our state.
> So now we are inviting you to celebrate with us.
> If you like what we are doing, just step up on the bus.
> Pick an issue needing fixing or a wrong that needs a right
> And, working all together, we'll bring it to the light.

The League of Women Voters was borne of the suffrage movement, so this commemoration of courageous women begins with glimpses of those leaders in the seventy-plus-year effort to gain the right to vote. One such leader was Iowan Carrie Chapman Catt, who founded the League of Women Voters to provide instruction about the structure and function of government to prepare women for informed voting. In the words of President Franklin Delano Roosevelt, "Democracy cannot succeed unless those who express their choice are prepared to choose wisely. The real safeguard of democracy, therefore, is education."

Mrs. Catt and the national League Board leaders then designed a method for data-based study of issues facing decision-makers in government. The process was, and remains, nonpartisan and leads to League position statements that underlie action by League members at national, state, and local levels of government. As anthropologist Margaret Mead said, "Never doubt that a small group of thoughtful committed citizens can change the world; indeed, it is the only thing that ever has."

The result of this action has impacted laws, policies, and practices at all levels of government in multiple areas, such as services for children and families, education, the environment, good government, human rights, and voting rights.

The primary focus of this centennial history of the League of Women Voters of Iowa and local League affiliates is to:

1. Honor the multitude of *people* who have given of their time and talents to improve government across one hundred years;
2. Explain the process of *study and action*, the foundation for League activities; and
3. Acknowledge the *products* of their labors.

It is hoped the reader will fully understand the title of the book— *And They Persisted*—and what is needed to counter the "slower than molasses" workings of government and the natural resistance of humans to change. Chapters 2–6 are a chronological history; other chapters do not need to be read in sequence. To help new members learn about the League's processes, Chapters 5, 6, and 9 are useful. For high school civics teachers, these same chapters are informative, as are Chapters 7, 8, and 11. There are occasional linkages to past events and perspectives on today's issues and future needs.

Appendices provide a myriad of additional information and resources. An effort has been made to be as accurate as possible, a challenge at times due to lack of historical records.

It's been a joy to compile! May it meet the goals of honoring and informing!

—L. Meloy

AND YOU REALLY THINK YOU'D LIKE TO ADOPT THIS ONE, TOO, MADAM?

"Ding" Darling cartoon from March 10, 1907. *"And you really think you'd like to adopt this one, too, Madam?"* Permission granted by the University of Iowa Photo Archives and the "Ding" Darling Wildlife Society.

Chapter 1

Stepping Up to a Challenge …

Preserving "One Person, One Vote"

"I DON'T KNOW, we have never done anything like this before!"
"Well, we have studied it for more years and in more depth than anyone else in the state!"
"Yes, but do we want the publicity if we fail?"
"It may ruin our nonpartisan reputation."
"What's it going to cost? Lawyers are not cheap."
"It's time to decide. I will call the roll."

Who were the people quoted above and what decision did they have to make?

It was April 1971 and thirteen state board members of the League of Women Voters of Iowa, under the leadership of President Jean Lloyd-Jones, were on a conference call from Mrs. Lloyd-Jones' Iowa City kitchen. They were discussing whether to join the Democratic Party, the Iowa Federation of Labor, and the Iowa Civil Liberties Union in a petition to the Iowa Supreme Court to review, and hopefully overturn, the state redistricting plan resulting from 1970 U.S. census data. Those three organizations wanted the Iowa League to join them partly because the League was known to be an authority on redistricting and partly because of the nonpartisan credibility of the League.

Why was the League considering joining the petition?

The Iowa League had studied reapportionment since 1955 and in 1963 adopted a position calling for a bipartisan, non-legislative redistricting authority. The League had also been instrumental in pushing a state-wide referendum in 1968 that adopted Iowa constitutional provisions

1

on reapportionment, with this very important directive: Any qualified elector had the right to appeal the Legislature-created plan to the Iowa Supreme Court. If the court found the plan unconstitutional, the court would adopt a plan within 90 days.

What had been done to prompt a possible petition to the Iowa Supreme Court?

Mary Garst of Coon Rapids and Betty Kitzman of Ames were part of the League's highly respected lobbying team and were known to be experts on reapportionment. Even though the Republican-controlled Legislature had adopted a plan that appeared to meet constitutional muster, Mrs. Garst and Mrs. Kitzman had inside information that some districts had been gerrymandered to protect incumbents (see gerrymandering in Glossary Appendix). Staff members in the Legislative Service Bureau—the agency charged with creating the plan—had divulged that several legislators had "just happened to stop by to look at the plan as it was being drawn and suggested moving lines just a bit" so that their districts would not be broken up.

Frank Miller cartoon, "Reapportionment." Permission granted by the *Des Moines Register*.

What did the LWVIA Board members decide that spring evening in 1971?

Mrs. Garst and Mrs. Kitzman argued forcefully that the League should join the petition. President Lloyd-Jones called the roll: Diana Bryant of Waterloo "yes," Marlys DeWild and Olive VanderWald of Pella "no," Louise Moon of Des Moines, Mrs. Garst, and Mrs. Kitzman "yes." At the end, with twelve board members voting, there were six "yes" and six "no" votes. President Lloyd-Jones cast the deciding vote, and the League joined the three organizations in the petition challenging the reapportionment plan. The phone call had lasted an hour at a cost of $131, money that was not in the League's budget.

To assist in the effort, Mrs. Garst and Mrs. Kitzman produced a reapportionment map that had virtually equal districts, with a lower population deviation than the legislators' plan and without adjustments for incumbents' current district configurations. They accomplished the work at Kirkwood Community College in Cedar Rapids on a mainframe computer that took up a whole room. Richard Bender, a friend of Mrs. Kitzman's from Ames who could have been called a "computer nerd," entered the parameters for problem-solving. President Lloyd-Jones noted that "every scrap of mimeographed paper the League had ever produced on reapportionment was introduced as evidence." (Google "mimeograph machine" if you haven't had the pleasure of getting mimeo fluid off your clothing.)

What happened with the petition to the Iowa Supreme Court?

Over fifty League members from twelve local Leagues attended the January 11, 1972, judicial hearing, as did representatives from the other three organizations. "Chief Justice C. Edwin Moore's opening remarks confirmed rumors that the justices had spent a great deal of time studying the briefs. He said they considered the case to be of utmost importance …" (*LWV of Iowa Voter*).

Mrs. Kitzman, sometimes called "Mrs. Reapportionment," was the star witness at the court hearing. Her testimony was concise and accurate, with just the right touch of humor. In cross-examination, the defendants' attorney asked, "Mrs. Kitzman, did you ever think of having a Republican on your committee?" She smiled and said, "Sir, I am a Republican." Obviously frustrated, he sputtered, "But you're an impartial Republican." Even Justice Moore had a hard time keeping a straight face.

Lead attorney Robert Fulton asserted that the Legislature had ignored the court's direction and had deliberately drawn district lines to maximize the political advantage of rural populations. An elaborate statistical explanation by Mr. Bender showed the chance of such a result on a purely random basis was 1,000 to 1. Attorney Dan Johnston then presented the League plan and asked that it be adopted. He also asked the court to grant payment of the applicants' expenses.

The opposition argued that voters were attached to their familiar district lines, the applicants were "nitpicking" and the whole case was "silly," adding that census data is not reliable. This apparent lack of faith in record-keeping and statistical analysis can still be heard today.

On January 14, the court handed down its unanimous opinion that the Legislature's plan violated both the Iowa and U.S. constitutions. In regard to the League's plan, the court indicated: "The relevance of the

League of Women Voters plan is not its availability as an alternate plan but rather its demonstration of applicants' principal thesis: namely, that plans more equal in population can be developed … Although we consider the efforts of the League laudable, and its plan relevant, it remains our duty to develop a decennial plan in keeping with the constitutional mandate." The ruling reflected another aspect of the constitutional amendment, "… if the plan is found unconstitutional, the Iowa Supreme Court will reapportion the state."

In spite of ten-below-zero temperatures, "there was dancing in the streets" of Des Moines that day, not just by League members, but by the supporters of the other three organizations and interested citizens who were reassured that 1) a citizen group made up of qualified electors could challenge a redistricting plan, and 2) the Iowa Supreme Court would come down hard on a legislature's attempt to violate the law to help incumbents win elections.

Note: The court denied applicants' expenses, so the League had to find the money to pay its portion of the legal fees. To do so, the League asked members in the thirty-six local Leagues for a donation of fifty cents per member. The money poured in, and the League met its obligations. Leaguers came through as they always have and still do!

Frank Miller cartoon, "The Old Grouch Wants Me to be Fair." January 23, 1972. Permission granted by the *Des Moines Register*.

While pleased with the League's efforts in challenging gerrymandering, President Lloyd-Jones, in her LWVIA president's farewell communication to Iowa Leagues in 1974, put the victory in perspective: "Big, dramatic court cases are exciting, but most progress [to impact change in government] is made by the day in, day out vigilance of people who know their job."

What has been the history of Iowa's reapportionment and redistricting plans since 1972?

In the four decades since this victory of "one man, one vote" in Iowa, there has not been another court challenge of the reapportionment plans prepared by the Legislative Services Agency (LSA), the nonpartisan professional research and service arm of the Legislature. A law passed in 1981 assigned the duty of preparing reapportionment plans to the LSA. Other aspects of that bill included the establishment of a timeline for consideration of up to three plans if necessary; anti-gerrymandering standards and measurements as guidelines to the LSA in preparation of a plan (see Reapportionment in Iowa Appendix); a bipartisan five-member Temporary Redistricting Advisory Commission appointed by legislative leaders to advise the LSA and conduct public hearings on the first plan; up-or-down votes without amendment on Plan 1 and Plan 2, with legislative direction to be given to the LSA for preparation of subsequent plans; and Plan 3 open to amendment from the floor.

In 1981, when 1980 census data was available and it was time for a new redistricting plan for Iowa, Mrs. Lloyd-Jones was a member of the Iowa House of Representatives. When the first plan had been voted down and the second agreed to, she asked Speaker of the House Don Avenson why the Legislature didn't go to a third plan, which could have been amended by the Legislature but perhaps would not have passed constitutional scrutiny. He replied, "Because they're afraid the League of Women Voters will take them to court again!"

What is the significance of the Iowa reapportionment process?

The Iowa redistricting plan is lauded by political scientists across the nation and is the envy of other states because:

- There is no gerrymandering of districts to protect incumbents;
- Voters can better understand their political address, i.e. voting district, because Iowa House, Senate, and congressional districts are aligned; and
- Deadlines for district creation allow for the process to be completed early in an election cycle to lessen candidate and voter confusion.

Currently, in thirty-seven states, legislatures are primarily responsible for legislative redistricting, typically adopting district lines by a simple majority vote in each chamber. In addition, governors usually have veto power. In these states, a majority party could easily gerrymander districts.

Why begin this centennial history of the League of Women Voters of Iowa with a chapter on reapportionment and redistricting?

The League's involvement in the creation of the Iowa redistricting process via a constitutional amendment and statutory law is one of its premier achievements across the almost one hundred years of League study and action in Iowa. The challenge to the redistricting plan in 1972 illustrates the power of action taken by informed citizens for the protection of rights. It also shows that involvement in the legislative process can promote new and better ways for government to serve its citizens.

More of the League's legislative work on behalf of all Iowans is presented in Chapter 8, following six chapters that provide the story of the suffrage movement, the passage of the Nineteenth Amendment, and the creation of the League with its principles and processes. That legislative chapter is a narrative, but an appendix is included for a quick-reference chronological listing of legislation by year and title or purpose. Readers will discover that the League has consistently been invested in improving the lives of citizens and their families on issues that range from health to education, protecting the environment, devising methods to make government more effective and efficient, and working to ensure human and voting rights.

Chapter 2

In the Beginning …

The First Women's Rights Advocates, Followed by the Suffrage Movement

"The long, hard work of reformers can lead to progress and a broader understanding of who is included in the phrase 'We, the People' … that work unfolds still." (1)

THE LEAGUE OF WOMEN VOTERS was born of the suffrage movement and was the grandchild of abolitionists, the latter champions of women's rights as well. Countless individuals worked unselfishly to rid this country of slavery and then to enfranchise women during decades of American history when communication and transportation were difficult and labor-saving devices for the home nonexistent. Most of these progressive or visionary people, women and men, remain nameless in historical accounts: laundresses to librarians, nannies to news carriers, seamstresses to secretaries, on farms and in factories, in small towns and seats of government, on the plains and in plazas.

A little-known Agency, Iowa, suffragist (read about Helen Nancy Beall Reed under Iowa suffragists in Chapter 2 Appendix).

Many of the leaders of both these historically significant movements are well known, with books written about them and foundations honoring their work. Some are even commemorated on U.S. currency, such as abolitionists Lucretia Mott and Sojourner Truth, along with suffragists Susan B. Anthony, Elizabeth Cady Stanton, and Alice Paul, who were chosen to be depicted on $10 and $20 bills sometime in the future.

In addition to their passion for increasing the rights of women, these past leaders for societal change exhibit many other commonalities. An investigation of their backgrounds and personal characteristics reveals their strengths—strengths also seen in League members across the almost one hundred years of League work to improve the lives of Iowans.

Commonalities of Abolitionists who Embraced Women's Suffrage

Many women—white and African American—who worked long and hard for the goal of abolition in the first half of the nineteenth century and later moved on to women's suffrage were highly educated for the time, attending boarding schools or studying with private tutors. Some, like Elizabeth Chandler and Abby Kelley, came from Quaker families who supported women's education and charitable work, particularly for the benefit of children, the poor, and the sick. Many came from activist families, such as the Fortens in Philadelphia; a few came from wealth; and several women were the daughters or wives of lawyers, or became lawyers themselves, as Mary Ann Shadd Cary did in the 1870s. They understood the power of organization and built substantial networks, working with others to strengthen the movement and achieve their goals. Women such as Julia Ward Howe, who collaborated for years with Lucy Stone, a later period suffragist, and Lydia Child, who worked tirelessly to expand her political connections, knew that only by standing together could women hope to achieve political equality. Female activists had the specific skills required for communicating a movement's message. Sarah and Angelina Grimke were outstanding speakers: "I know nothing of men's rights, or women's rights, human rights are all that I recognize." Susan B. Anthony supported herself much of her life through public speaking. Suffragists also communicated through newspapers during a period when travel may have been impossible for many. Thus, many of these activists were writers and editors, such as Frances Watkins Harper and scholar Anna Julia Cooper. Mrs. Cooper's statement, "The cause of freedom is not the cause of a race or a sect, a party, or a class—it is the cause of humankind, the birthright of humanity," was placed on pages 24 and 25 of the 2016 U.S. passport. Many abolitionists and suffragists also were prolific letter writers, honing their writing skills to convince and encourage.

In addition to speaking and writing skills called linguistic intelligence or word smarts (2), many suffragists also possessed strong organizational abilities (logical-mathematical intelligence or reasoning smarts). Susan B. Anthony, known for organizing suffrage conventions and campaigns and for lobbying Congress and state legislatures on suffrage issues, was recognized as one of the senior political figures in the United States after the Civil War for her interpersonal intelligence or people smarts. Sojourner Truth, whose personal magnetism was noted by many who knew and worked with her, probably possessed interpersonal intelligence as well.

Some suffrage activists were artistic or creative: Lydia Child wrote children's books and the Thanksgiving poem "Over the River and Through the Wood"; Elizabeth Margaret Chandler wrote the poem "The Slave Ship" and many other works; Julia Ward Howe wrote the lyrics for the "Battle Hymn of the Republic" in 1861; and Sarah Forten Purvis was a poet, with "The Grave of the Slave" an example of her early published work.

In addition to being activists for abolition and then suffrage, most of these women were unconventional for their times and were not afraid to take positions counter to social mores. For example, Abby Kelley gave a public speech in 1838 that was labeled "promiscuous" because both men and women were in the audience, a double whammy because women were not supposed to speak in public, let alone to men! Lydia Child spoke out against churches' subjugation of women and was an advocate for the rights of Native Americans, the latter fairly unheard of in the mid-nineteenth century.

These women were "ahead of the times," a founding principle of the League of Women Voters. And, their personal characteristics are similar to those of Iowa League members in the past and present: hard working, goal oriented, and accomplished organizers with excellent communication skills. As Minnette Doderer (1923–2005), a Johnson County Leaguer, Iowa's longest-serving female legislator, and a 1979 inductee into the Iowa Women's Hall of Fame, stated: "I joined the League because I thought it was the greatest organization with all those smart women!"

Suffrage Organizations

The passage of the Thirteenth Amendment, ratified December 6, 1865, triggered women's transition from abolitionist activism to singular support of suffrage organizations. The American Equal Rights Association (AERA), dedicated to suffrage for both black men and all women, and the New England Woman Suffrage Association (NEWSA) came into existence first, followed several years later by the National Woman Suffrage Association (NWSA) and the American Woman Suffrage Association (AWSA), rival groups that merged in 1890 to form the National American Woman Suffrage Association (NAWSA). These organizations had different operating strategies, varied in structure, and were led by women with differing management styles, political alliances and collaborations, and ideologies.

As in any movement for change, there was controversy across the nearly seventy years of organized efforts to gain women the right to vote, evidenced by battles for leadership and disagreements over alliances, strategies, and prioritization of movement goals. Across those same years, social and political realities impacted the populace as a whole and influenced decision-makers in state and federal governments.

The vast majority of women, whether black or white, did not belong to any suffrage organization. Many women nevertheless gained familiarity with the movement's message through reading women's suffrage articles in newspapers and magazines, attending community events featuring suffrage speakers, and joining other groups that supported enhanced public roles for women, such as the Woman's Christian Temperance Union (WCTU) and other women's clubs (see Glossary Appendix).

Lisa Tetrault, in *The Myth of Seneca Falls: Memory and the Women's Suffrage Movement, 1848–1898*, states it well:

> Movements can and do begin in many places. One could anchor the beginning of the women's rights movement in the U.S. in many events … One could begin with the Grimke sisters' practical and theoretical defenses of women as public actors in the 1830s. With black women's resistance to slavery and to the systematic raping of their bodies. With the Lowell Mill textile operatives and their 1834 and 1836 strikes for fair treatment and decent wages. With the early anatomy lectures of Mary Gove Nichols and Paulina Wright (Davis) that helped women claim sovereignty over their bodies. With six women in upstate New York who, in 1846, two years before [the] Seneca Falls [gathering in 1848] (where the first demand for female enfranchisement was supposedly made), petitioned their state constitutional convention for the right to vote. With Lucy Stone's 1847 lecture tour on women's rights. With the first national women's rights convention in Worcester, MA, in 1850, when local events became coordinated into a larger, national whole. Or on a smaller scale, with the moment any given individual woman chose to enter a life of activism on behalf of

her sex. Women's rights had many beginnings. And for much of the early to mid-nineteenth century, people commonly invoked a variety of events when they spoke about the origins of women's rights." (3)

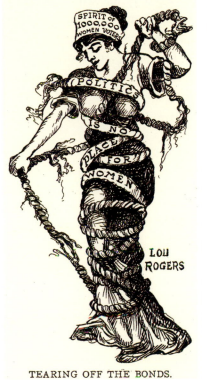

"Tearing Off the Bonds" cartoon by Annie Lucasta "Lou" Rogers.

TEARING OFF THE BONDS.

Commonalities of Suffragists who Led National Organizations

The women identified with the suffrage movement from 1850 to 1920, like those women in the abolition movement, were well-educated. Some came from activist families, such as Matilda Joslyn Gage, whose New York childhood home had been a station on the Underground Railroad. Many came from wealth or had fathers or husbands who were lawyers. Others, like Alice Paul, earned their own law degrees. As with the abolitionists, the suffragists networked with others in the movement, through correspondence, personal visits if travel was possible, and attendance at public events and suffrage association meetings. For example, Susan B. Anthony and Elizabeth Cady Stanton collaborated on articles and speeches (usually in Mrs. Stanton's home because she had small children). Susan B. Anthony also had connections, along with other suffragists, to Lucy Stone, M.J. Gage, Anna Shaw, and the eventual League founder Carrie Chapman Catt. And many suffragists were close friends, such as Elizabeth Boynton Harbert and Iowan Annie Savery. Mrs. Savery also was a friend of Amelia Bloomer, another Iowan.

The suffragists also possessed the skills needed to communicate with the public about the rationale for expanding women's rights, and in particular, the right to vote. Many had excellent oral communication skills and traveled the country speaking publicly on women's suffrage. Anna Howard Shaw, for instance, was an exceptional orator. Her June 1915 speech, "The Fundamental Principles of a Republic," ranks twenty-seventh in American Rhetoric's "Top 100 Speeches." (4) Mrs. Catt also was a powerful speaker. As a college freshman, she began a literary society speech with this forceful argument: "How is it possible that a woman who is unfit to vote should be the mother of, and bring up, a man who is?"

Because radio was not available until after the Nineteenth Amendment became the law of the land, suffragists used newspapers and magazines to reach the public. Many suffragists were excellent writers, journalists, or editors. Examples include Josephine Ruffin and her *Woman's Era*, the first newspaper published by and for African American women, and Gertrude Bustill Mossell, who wrote for the *New York Freeman* urging women to read the history of the suffrage movement and called for a federal amendment to enfranchise women in 1885.

Due to their education levels, we can assume that these leaders of the suffrage movement had higher than average intelligence. Again, applying Howard Gardner's varying types of intelligence, many speakers, writers, and editors mentioned above possessed linguistic intelligence. Other suffragists probably had equally important intelligences that aided the movement in these two areas of ability:

> 1. Logical-mathematical (skills for organizing), evidenced by Mary Church Terrell not only in her work for suffrage but also in her organization of the National Association of Colored Women in 1896 and co-founding of the National Association for the Advancement of Colored People (NAACP) in 1901. Alice Paul was the principal organizer of the 1913 Woman Suffrage Parade in Washington, D.C., where 8,000 suffragists from all over the country marched on the day of President Woodrow Wilson's inauguration—now that's organizing!

> 2. Interpersonal (skills motivating others), evidenced by the oration and motivation skills of Lucy Stone, who in the 1850s traveled the United States and Canada, speaking for abolition and women's rights, out-earning many men on the lecture circuit. Despite often being initially heckled, her end result with most audiences was support for her cause. Many women ad-

mired her for not taking her husband's last name, which was expected in those times, and for the public acknowledgement of her and her husband's unconventional marriage vows. The vows were, in fact, a civil protest of the lack of control women had over themselves, their children, and their property, along with their lack of legal status when married.

Also, many suffragists could be described as artistic or creative: Elizabeth Boynton Harbert wrote poems and songs as a child and young adult, and three novels later in her life. She also is an example of the multitalented nature of many gifted women in the suffrage movement. Along with being a well-known author, she was an exceptional orator and a suffrage organizer, serving as president of the Iowa Woman Suffrage Association. She also must have possessed "people smarts" in that she was the first woman to design and secure a women's rights plank in a major political party's state platform (Iowa Republican Party in 1874).

Matilda Fletcher traveled alone by coach and train throughout the Midwest, lecturing on education reform, temperance, and suffrage. She was known as a powerful speaker, so much so that a man supposedly named a silver mine after her! Like other suffragists, she had to be creative to meet the demands of her work, so she designed and patented a traveling trunk, which was innovative for the time and helped make her travel easier.

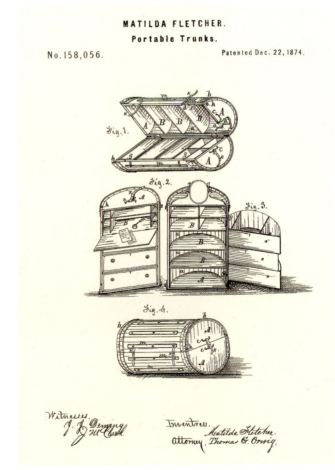

Matilda Fletcher's diagram of the traveling trunk she designed.

Like the multitalented Mrs. Harbert and Ms. Fletcher, many other leaders of the suffrage movement possessed above average intellectual capacity but also many talents suited for the movement. One of those women was Iowan Carrie Chapman Catt, a major force for the passage of the Nineteenth Amendment and the founder of the League of Women Voters. Much has been written about Mrs. Catt and many honors bestowed, including a 1948 U.S. postage stamp of the Seneca Falls Convention (with Elizabeth Cady Stanton and Lucretia Mott); induction into the Iowa and national women's halls of fame; and the establishment of the Carrie Chapman Catt Center for Women and Politics at Iowa State University.

Carrie Chapman Catt as president of the National American Woman Suffrage Association, 1900–1904, State Historical Society of Iowa.

Mrs. Catt was a fine writer, as evidenced by her "Woman's World" columns for her first husband's Mason City newspaper and her 1923 book, *Women Suffrage and Politics: The Inner Story of the Suffrage Movement*. She was also a gifted speaker. After she began lecturing on women's voting rights in 1887, observers consistently described her efforts as scholarly, witty, and convincing.

Mrs. Catt used her organizational skills to form small suffrage groups in Iowa and neighboring states as well as to lead the national organization. Her methods relied on education and strategic tactics to reach the goal of universal women's suffrage. Her "Winning Plan" was a coordination of state suffrage organizations to win the vote through legislatures, state by state.

And, as a realist, when the state-by-state approach did not yield the desired results, particularly after the June 1916 referendum loss in her home state of Iowa, Mrs. Catt designed a new strategic plan to secure a constitutional amendment for women's suffrage, which became the Nineteenth Amendment.

1916 Iowa Vote billboard, State Historical Society of Iowa.

Always looking at future needs, Mrs. Catt wanted to ensure that enfranchised women were prepared to be conscientious voters. So, she designed a citizenship curriculum used first for her suffrage workers and ultimately to educate the public (see Chapter 5). She also created an organization to train newly-enfranchised women, or others such as immigrants, in the workings of government and in the investigation of issues that decision-makers would be addressing. That organization was the League of Women Voters, which Mrs. Catt founded in 1920 after the passage of the Nineteenth Amendment. She thought it would be needed for just a few years. But, aren't we glad she was wrong about its longevity? (Chapter 2 Appendix contains more information on Mrs.

Catt, her life, and accomplishments, particularly her strategic management of the last twenty years of the work to gain women's suffrage.)

Like Mrs. Catt above, many of the suffragists also were "ahead of their times," initially because they supported a movement that, antisuffragists argued, would destroy families and negatively impact society in other ways (see Chapter 3). And some of these women were unconventional for other reasons: Matilda Joslyn Gage advocated, along with Mrs. Stanton, for a woman's right to control her own body with respect to sexual activity and the bearing of children, and she was an early opponent of human trafficking, still a concern in 2020. Ms. Gage's writing on the lack of equity in the evaluations of the work of men versus that of women came to be known as the "Matilda Effect," a social situation where women receive less credit for their work than an objective examination would reveal. Another suffragist, physician Verina Morton Jones, led the way in regard to childcare for children of working parents when she established a day nursery and free kindergarten in 1908 in a Brooklyn settlement house.

Iowa Pioneer Suffragists

"Lock the Granary, Peggy!"
So lock the granary Peggy, and make the hencoop stout,
Put the hogs back in the orchard, and turn the cattle out,
Hide the horses on the hillside, and should the assessor come

We'll lock the door and make believe the folks are not at home.
The women then we'll rally, for this is woman's cause,
We'll tell them that we've learned a way to aid in making laws.
We'll do no work but only sing and shout from the roof and steeple,

We'll cook your meals and pay our tax, when you admit that we are people. (5)

The characteristics shared by female abolitionists and those who led national suffrage organizations also apply to suffragists in Iowa. The Iowa women were well-educated, and some had advanced degrees. Laetitia Conard from Grinnell earned a Ph.D. in 1869, and entomologist Hortense Butler Heywood of Cherokee wrote her own books that included her drawings of the insects she studied.

Several of the Iowa suffragists had husbands who were lawyers, with two of them, Annie Savery and Arabella Mansfield, earning law degrees themselves. Several came from Quaker backgrounds or had activist parents, such as Mary Adams, whose parents were abolitionists. Some women came from family wealth or had entrepreneurial spouses, such as Martha Callanan. She equated an individual's wealth with responsi-

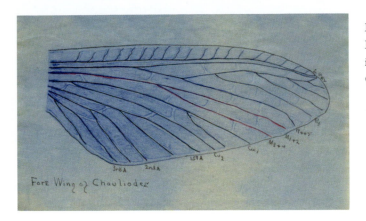

Entomologist Hortense Butler Heywood's drawing of the fore wing of Chauliodes.

bilities for the betterment of humanity through one's time and energy. That philosophy is well represented in the work she and her husband accomplished in Des Moines and beyond (see Chapter 4 Appendix). And all the Iowa suffragists had special skills needed in the suffrage movement. Amelia Bloomer, Mary Darwin, Martha Callanan, Mary Adams, and Rowena Stevens were excellent public speakers (linguistic intelligence), as were Mary Jane Coggeshall and Annie Savery.

Many of the Iowa suffragists had logical-mathematical intelligence, evidenced in their superb organizing skills: Flora Dunlap, first president of the League of Women Voters (see Chapter 6); Annie Lawther, who went on to be the first woman appointed to the Iowa Board of Education; and Vivian Smith, who was the suffrage chair for the Iowa Federation of Colored Women's Clubs.

Iowa Landscape for Women's Rights Reformers in Late 1800s, Early 1900s

WOMEN'S RIGHTS

The Iowa Code of 1851 enacted some of the most progressive laws in the nation relating to married women's property rights. Married women could own property as long as they registered it in their own names at the county recorder's office within five years of acquisition. In 1870, the General Assembly extended to married women the same rights to enter into contracts as unmarried women had always held. Later, the Code of 1873 firmly established the right of married women to their own wages. In the area of divorce, after Iowa gained statehood in 1846, all divorce cases were heard by the district courts. Women, and men, could seek divorce only if they could prove the existence of one of a legally specified set of causes; women filing for divorce frequently invoked the charge of "cruel or inhumane treatment." Until 1889, such cruelty had to be manifested physically, but a ruling handed down that year determined that mental cruelty could form the basis for a divorce petition as well.

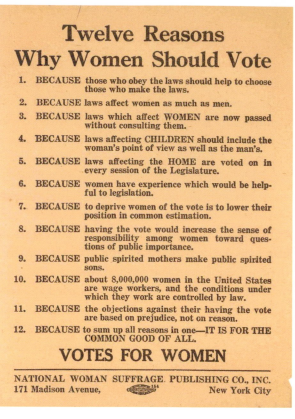

Twelve Reasons Why Women Should Vote

1. BECAUSE those who obey the laws should help to choose those who make the laws.
2. BECAUSE laws affect women as much as men.
3. BECAUSE laws which affect WOMEN are now passed without consulting them.
4. BECAUSE laws affecting CHILDREN should include the woman's point of view as well as the man's.
5. BECAUSE laws affecting the HOME are voted on in every session of the Legislature.
6. BECAUSE women have experience which would be helpful to legislation.
7. BECAUSE to deprive women of the vote is to lower their position in common estimation.
8. BECAUSE having the vote would increase the sense of responsibility among women toward questions of public importance.
9. BECAUSE public spirited mothers make public spirited sons.
10. BECAUSE about 8,000,000 women in the United States are wage workers, and the conditions under which they work are controlled by law.
11. BECAUSE the objections against their having the vote are based on prejudice, not on reason.
12. BECAUSE to sum up all reasons in one—IT IS FOR THE COMMON GOOD OF ALL.

VOTES FOR WOMEN

NATIONAL WOMAN SUFFRAGE PUBLISHING CO., INC.
171 Madison Avenue,   New York City

With respect to children, the Code of 1851 identified the father as the natural guardian of his minor children. Not until 1873 was the Iowa Code changed to vest both parents with equal rights of guardianship. Women in Iowa did not gain the right to vote in general elections until the passage of the Nineteenth Amendment in 1920. However, in 1894, Iowa's General Assembly passed legislation that gave women the right to vote in municipal and school elections that involved the issuing of bonds, borrowing money, or increasing taxes. (6)

ISOLATION

From the state's earliest history, as female reformers sought to correct legal and political inequities, they faced numerous obstacles. One of the most daunting hurdles was the isolation women often encountered in largely rural Iowa. In the state's early years, female activists struggled to simply get from place to place. When Amelia Bloomer and her husband moved from Ohio to Council Bluffs in 1855, their journey to the sparsely-populated western part of the state required three legs: a train to St. Louis, a riverboat to St. Joseph, Missouri, and then an exhausting stagecoach journey to Council Bluffs. Not until 1867 did the first railroad, the Chicago and North Western, complete a route from the

Mississippi River to the Missouri River. Even with this progress, most communities in the state had to wait until the 1880s—the decade of greatest growth in Iowa railroading—for branch lines to incorporate them into the state's railroad network (see Chapter 4 Appendix for Des Moines businessmen married to suffragists who were involved in expanding railways in Iowa). The railroads brought dependable, year-round transportation that made travel for business or pleasure possible across the state and region. Later, in the early twentieth century, suffragists used newly mass-produced automobiles in parades and cross-country tours to promote their cause if their family income allowed for such a purchase. (7)

TRAVEL

Although advances in transportation helped lessen rural women's social isolation, traveling away from home still was not an option for many Iowa women because of health issues, family and farm responsibilities, or financial limitations. Women in these situations found other ways to develop connections, such as supporting traveling orators who spoke in favor of reform. As early as 1854, Frances Dana Gage, a writer and women's rights pioneer, lectured in the southeastern part of the state. Amelia Bloomer presented women's rights lectures in Council Bluffs within months of her arrival. After the Civil War, the lecture circuit expanded dramatically, and women began to gain widespread acceptance as authoritative speakers. The best-known of them could command handsome fees, such as Susan B. Anthony. Hundreds of female orators crisscrossed the nation in the latter decades of the nineteenth century, making stops in cities and towns across the Midwest, and many of them spoke in favor of women's rights. These lectures not only provided educational resources but also exposed female audience members to like-minded individuals in their communities and provided opportunities for organization in pursuit of reform. (8)

COMMUNICATION

Women also took advantage of the postal service to build networks and share ideas. In the face of prohibitively expensive or difficult travel, female suffrage activists had long sent correspondence to women's rights conventions as a way to demonstrate their support. At the first national women's rights convention in Worcester, Massachusetts, in 1850, advocates who could not attend wrote letters in support of women's dress and marriage reform and women's right to participate in government. Postal correspondence became an even more attractive option when, in 1872, the federal government issued its first official postal card. For the price of one cent, this new form of communication gave every woman, no matter where she lived, the opportunity to express her views to movement leaders in far-off cities. In 1880, Elizabeth Cady Stanton took advantage of the one-cent postal card and sought correspondence from women nationwide as proof of their fervent interest in gaining the ballot. Four hundred and sixty-nine Iowa women responded to Mrs. Stanton's call; from Burlington to Decorah to Storm Lake, women across the state voiced their desire to vote. Thus the postal service helped alleviate rural isolation by providing women the opportunity to communicate with activists in the next town or across the nation.

Newspapers also provided women with a forum to express their sentiments for reform. Women like Amelia Bloomer launched their own newspapers—Mrs. Bloomer's *The Lily* debuted in 1849 as a temperance paper but later became a mouthpiece for women's rights—while others contributed letters and articles advocating reforms to mainstream newspapers. The years 1870 to 1890 were particularly prolific for the suffrage press. Women contributed, as publishers, writers and readers, to suffrage newspapers that brought the discussion of women's political equality to larger and larger audiences. Newspaper articles supporting women's rights reached a less homogenous readership than did suffrage lecturers and convention speakers. For farm women in particular, these newspaper articles helped establish a common identity as potentially effective agents of change, allowing them to envision themselves as active members of the movement. The *Woman's Standard*, a monthly newspaper produced by the Iowa Woman Suffrage Association, distributed two thousand copies to four hundred towns in 1901! The *Standard* used farm-based rhetorical appeals and included updates on suffrage work in rural areas to raise farm women's consciousness and give them a voice in the movement. (9)

DOMESTICITY

During the time period of the suffrage movement, for the majority of men and women, society had two spheres: the public one, controlled by men, and the private one of the home, dominated by women. In addition to their child-rearing responsibilities, women performed unpaid domestic tasks such as cooking, cleaning, sewing, and laundry. Farm women had the additional responsibilities of growing and preserving food, as well as caring for and processing animals used for food.

In Iowa, where half the population lived on farms in the late nineteenth century, housewives had few labor-saving devices at their disposal. Water needed for laundry, cleaning, bathing, and cooking had to be carried into the home from a pump in the yard. The stoves used for cooking required a constant supply of wood. As cooks today know, preparing three meals per day from scratch is time-consuming, and though prepared foods were available in tins and jars, they were expensive and perhaps not available in rural areas. Most women owned few cleaning tools beyond brooms and rug beaters. A carpet sweeper was invented in 1876 but may have been too costly for rural households. It also was of no use in homes with just wood floors or linoleum, which had been available since the 1860s.

To meet the clothing needs of a family, many rural households owned treadle sewing machines, operated manually by pushing a foot pedal. Clothing could be purchased from a dress maker, though this would have been costly and perhaps not available in a rural setting. For laundering clothing, farm women used washboards in tubs and hung clothes to dry. The modern clothespin was invented in 1853 and was useful if one had a clothesline to attach it and the clothing to! Wringers or mangles were invented in 1850 and helped extract water from the washed clothes to hasten drying, but laundry remained back-breaking work. To press clothing on a portable ironing board, which was available as early as 1875, women had to heat a flat iron on the wood stove. Electric irons were not invented until electricity was available, first in cities and not until the mid-1900s in rural Iowa.

So, there was a massive amount of work to be done by women who lived in rural Iowa during the suffrage movement. That reality gave them little time to participate beyond reading magazine articles and newspaper opinion pieces, as well as talking to neighbors and friends at the few social events common in rural communities, often held at churches and schools.

Life for women of means, many of whom were active in the suffrage movement, was dramatically different. They had the same domestic responsibilities as less affluent women, but most likely had indoor running water and could afford domestic help for cooking, cleaning, sewing, and laundry, as well as childcare. Also, they would be better able to purchase labor-saving devices when available. Therefore, wealthy women had more time and energy to engage in the suffrage movement and became leaders of gaining the right to vote for all women.

SUFFRAGE LEADERSHIP

Two Des Moines residents, both married to entrepreneurial spouses, will be highlighted here: Mary Jane Coggeshall, identified by Carrie Chapman Catt as "The Mother of Woman Suffrage in Iowa," (10) and Annie Nowlin Savery, the prototype of a modern Leaguer.

Mary Jane Whiteley Coggeshall (1836–1911) was raised in Indiana as a Hicksite Quaker, arriving in Des Moines in 1865 with husband John, an Orthodox Quaker (at their marriage both were disowned due to being from different sects, though they "condemned their misconduct" later

Mary Jane Coggeshall, State
Historical Society of Iowa.

so he could rejoin his sect). He became a successful businessman, first
with a clothing store and later with other ventures, including serving as
an adjuster for Iowa Loan and Trust. He also worked with F.M. Hubbell
(ancestor of 2018 gubernatorial nominee Fred Hubbell) in securing
rights-of-way in the city for the Wabash Railroad.

While raising to adulthood five of seven children, Mrs. Coggeshall
got involved in women's suffrage in 1870 after joining the Polk County
Woman Suffrage Society. She became not only a force for change but
a gracious hostess. Historical records of her work do not include the
hundreds of county and state society committee meetings and parlor
meetings held in her home or the use of her spare bedroom for suffrage guests, nor food served from her table to suffrage workers. She
was editor of the *Woman's Hour* and then the *Woman's Standard*, along
with being a charter member of the Iowa Woman Suffrage Association,
serving as president in 1890–91 and in 1903–05. Beginning in 1894 and
for several years afterward she was a board member of the National
American Woman Suffrage Association. By 1897 there were eighty-five
county societies and 150 local clubs in Iowa dedicated to female enfran-
chisement. Mrs. Coggeshall reportedly said when planning suffrage
activities that marching was too radical and an un-ladylike approach.
But she did march in the 1908 Boone Suffrage Parade, the first in Iowa
and possibly first in the nation. She was right behind the all-male brass

band, followed by one hundred suffragists in town for the three-day thirty-seventh Iowa Equal Suffrage Association Convention: "My husband says that the parade today has done more to advance the cause of political equality in Boone than all the suffrage clubs, all the conventions, all the lectures and debates have ever done … there was but one topic of conversation that afternoon in the homes, shops, offices, and stores and on the street, and that was suffrage for women …" (11)

1908 Boone Suffrage Parade, State Historical Society of Iowa.

Mrs. Coggeshall was known for being logical and persuasive, and providing convincing arguments. She also was described as witty with beautiful diction. Her own eloquent words illustrate those strengths:

"Our protest is not against men. Our protest is against the system which men are born into. I could wish no better environment for my sons than that they might go out into the world where everyone of God's children has an equal chance. Let us put away from us the idea that this demand of the modern woman for full political freedom is the outburst of a few unbalanced minds. It began out of the political and religious revolution in Germany, France, Italy, and America simultaneously by women unknown to each other, their demand for a wider sphere of action in every civilized country."—1893 Equality Club address, Eagle Grove (12)

"… there are today 77,000 more women than men in our [nation's] high schools. The whole system of primary education is in the hands of women; and higher education is threatened with the same result. These teachers are expected to imbue the minds of their pupils with patriotism, and a love for the government. This government says to every high school woman that no matter how good or how learned she may become, her opinion will be of no account at the ballot box where her environment is decided. History has no precedent for absurdity like this."—October 6, 1903, Iowa Equal Suffrage Association Convention, Boone (13)

"I am no more interested in one sex than the other; the best years of my life have been spent in raising boys whose welfare is more dear to me than my life, and if we speak of the wrongs which the world practices towards women it is because these wrongs make life harder for both our boys and our girls. It has been well said that if women are not to be free, it was a fatal mistake that they were given the alphabet."—1894 "For What Purpose do We Live" article (14)

We who have toiled up the steps of the old Capitol only to see our bills defeated upon final vote. We who took our baby boys with us to those early meetings, now find these boys are voters, while their mothers are still asking for freedom. We only hope that the next generation of women may find their work made easier because we have trodden the path before them. (15)

"Women well-housed and fed with husbands and sons who are kind and considerate and good and just to women—why talk of liberty because that is what Americans do and we have the resources to help all women to live as we do, but also for all of us to have equal rights of property and the vote which even the most educated and affluent of us do not enjoy—yet!"—1896 Iowa Equal Suffrage Association Convention, Independence, Iowa (16)

This highly intelligent and gifted writer and orator did not live to see the passage of the Nineteenth Amendment. Following her death, the Iowa Woman Suffrage Association and the Men's League for Women's Suffrage set up the Mary J. Coggeshall Memorial Fund, whose mission was to support activities leading to the passage of a suffrage amendment to the Iowa Constitution. She may never have known that Carrie Chapman Catt thought her to be Mrs. Catt's greatest inspiration. In 1990, she was inducted into the Iowa Women's Hall of Fame. The Schlesinger Library of the Radcliffe Institute for Advanced Study at Harvard University has an archive of Mrs. Coggeshall's papers—mainly speeches and writings. Her great-nephew John N. (Jake) Ferris has penned a biography of his great-grandmother's sister, cited in References.

Annie Nowlin Savery, State Historical Society of Iowa.

Annie Nowlin Savery (1831–1891) was born in London and came to Des Moines as a child. She married land speculator and businessman James Savery in New York in 1853. In 1854, Mr. Savery built his first hotel, the Marvin House, which Mrs. Savery helped manage. In 1862, he built his second hotel, the Savery, now known as The Renaissance

Des Moines Savery Hotel. Having only a grade school education, Mrs. Savery began several years of self-education after their marriage, using the curriculum of the Des Moines public schools and employing private tutors for advanced study of Shakespeare, French, history, and religion. Frank Mills, a local bookstore owner, reported that Mrs. Savery had the finest library in the state at the time and was the best educated woman in Iowa.

Her beauty, kindness, and conversational skills made her popular in Des Moines social circles, but she possessed far more talents than those agreeable attributes. Along with being civic-minded and well-informed, Mrs. Savery was an excellent public speaker. In fact, in 1869 she became the first woman in Des Moines to speak publicly in support of women's rights—to an antagonistic male audience that she eventually won over, either through her rationale or her charm!

Mrs. Savery's friend Amelia Bloomer asked her to speak at the 1870 Iowa Woman Suffrage Association organizational meeting, after which she organized the Polk County Woman Suffrage Society. She continued to make speeches across Iowa and wrote suffrage essays for local newspapers.

In the 1870s, anti-suffrage groups used the free-love movement (see the Glossary Appendix) to attack suffragists, arguing that granting women the right to vote would destroy the institutions of marriage and family. The proponents of free-love encouraged women's expression of their sexuality at a time when much of society assigned to women no sexual feelings, only a maternal instinct for procreation. Mrs. Savery agreed with many of the free-love concepts but stated that because sexual expression was a private matter, it should not be part of a suffrage platform. Some in the suffrage movement thought it should be included. So, both proponents and opponents of the free-love movement criticized Mrs. Savery. In 1872, she and a group of suffragists got permission to speak in support of the second vote on a suffrage bill in the Iowa Legislature, but when they arrived, they were not allowed to speak. The legislators who had promised to vote in favor of the bill did not, and it was defeated that year.

At that point, Mrs. Savery was discouraged and "retired" from suffrage work, though she did not curl up in a ball in her magnificent library in their elegant home at Nineteenth and Grand. Instead, she picked herself up, dusted herself off, and went to law school! She graduated in 1875 from what would become the University of Iowa College of Law; she and another woman in her class were the first female law school graduates in the state. Mrs. Savery did not practice law but devoted the next fifteen years of her life to humanitarian pursuits. She was a founding member of the Des Moines Library Association; she established, at what would become Grinnell College, a scholarship program for girls and remained active in its administration; she was the first woman to visit the Polk County jail, identifying the deplorable conditions there and working with others to implement reforms; and she started a beekeeping business, the Iowa-Italian Bee Company, with nationally known apiarist Ellen Tupper as an example of possible economic independence for women.

The Saverys' home was destroyed by fire in 1874, about the same time that Mr. Savery faced financial disaster, prompting the couple to move to Montana for land acquisition opportunities. They returned to Des Moines in 1878, when Mr. Savery and James Callanan formed the American Emigrant Company. By 1883, the Saverys had a second home in New York City, dividing their time between it and Des Moines.

Annie Savery, inducted into the Iowa Women's Hall of Fame in 1997, was not only a self-educated person knowledgeable about her community and progressive in her approaches to problem-solving, but she was an orator and writer who influenced people's thinking. And like the leaders of the suffrage movement and members of the League of Women Voters, she was resilient after defeat and persevered.

Psychologist Angela Duckworth described the personality trait of persevering while facing struggles and obstacles in attaining a long-term goal as "grit." (17) The suffrage movement was certainly made up of lots of individuals with grit like Mrs. Savery. They had to face opposition to women's suffrage in many forms: harsh words both spoken and written; not being allowed to speak at public events and in front of government decision-makers; and even imprisonment for participation in marches and protests.

Many suffragists also had significant personal hardships. Iowans Mary Jane Coggeshall and Rowena Stevens, though women of means, still had children to raise—five and seven, respectively—along with their suffrage work. Julia Ward Howe endured a long and unhappy marriage. Elizabeth Cady Stanton found life as a housewife limiting and unstimulating. Ida B. Wells-Barnett endured her source of income, her newspaper, being destroyed by a white lynch mob. Vivian Smith could not make a living as a teacher in her hometown because she was black. Carrie Chapman Catt lost two husbands—Leo within one year of marriage and George after fifteen years of marriage. These women had grit and kept moving forward working for justice for women despite personal challenges. The League of Women Voters, as upcoming chapters will show, is an organization of individuals who also know how to persevere against struggles and obstacles in their quest to gain better policies and laws for the public good in Iowa. It's a group with grit!

The Chapter 2 Appendix provides short biographies of more than fifty women involved in the suffrage movement (some mentioned in "commonalities" above), some on the national level and others known for their work in Iowa. That appendix also contains resource lists for interested readers.

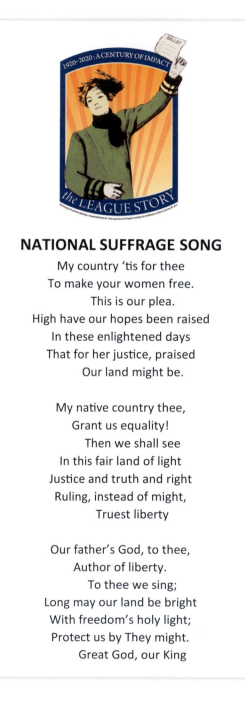

NATIONAL SUFFRAGE SONG

My country 'tis for thee
To make your women free.
This is our plea.
High have our hopes been raised
In these enlightened days
That for her justice, praised
Our land might be.

My native country thee,
Grant us equality!
Then we shall see
In this fair land of light
Justice and truth and right
Ruling, instead of might,
Truest liberty

Our father's God, to thee,
Author of liberty.
To thee we sing;
Long may our land be bright
With freedom's holy light;
Protect us by They might.
Great God, our King

Chapter 3

Hard Won …

The Nineteenth Amendment Becomes a Reality

The right of citizens of the United States to vote shall not be denied or abridged by the United States or by any State on account of sex. Congress shall have power to enforce this article by appropriate legislation.
—Nineteenth Amendment, U.S. Constitution

THE STORY OF UNIVERSAL women's suffrage in this country is a long one, more than seventy years, depending on which scholar's date you accept as its beginning. It is a story of the efforts of thousands of people and expenditures of millions of dollars.

In Iowa, it began formally in 1870 when Joseph Dugdale, a Quaker and former anti-slavery activist, called together a group of men and women to meet in Mount Pleasant to form the Iowa Woman Suffrage Association. Twelve hundred people attended the event. Amelia Bloomer and Annie Savery were two of the speakers (see Chapter 2 and its Appendix). After that gathering, local groups formed across the state and worked to change Iowa law to enfranchise women. Suffrage activists wrote letters and articles, made speeches, published leaflets and newspaper opinion pieces, and created songs, poems, and plays.

The first Iowa suffrage amendment was introduced in the General Assembly that same year and in every session thereafter through 1919, or forty-nine years. In 1900, women's suffrage groups presented a petition containing 100,000 signatures from a population of 2,231,853 to the General Assembly. It did not move the legislators to authorize a referendum for suffrage. Why did all the efforts of individuals working for suffrage fail to change Iowa law by 1900? Anti-suffrage groups played a significant role.

"Ding" Darling cartoon from February 20, 1909. "Once more the castle is being besieged." Permission granted by the University of Iowa Photo Archives and the "Ding" Darling Wildlife Society.

The Anti-Suffrage Movement

Formed in Washington, D.C., in 1870, the National Woman Anti-Suffrage Association provided money, literature, and speakers to state anti-suffrage campaigns. Iowa formed an anti-suffrage association that same year, though less formally organized than the national association.

It did not espouse public speaking by female members until the late 1890s because it was considered "unladylike." The Iowa anti-suffrage movement was led primarily by well-to-do wives, mothers, wage earners, and professional women. They became active when suffrage came up before the General Assembly, using pamphlets, largely Republican newspapers, and small parlor discussions with legislators to spread their message. (1)

Anti-suffragists believed that if women gained the right to vote, the whole social system of men controlling the public sphere would be overturned. Women managing the home and children, which was the well-established cultural gender role at the time, would no longer prevail. As a result of this perception, men formed anti-suffrage organizations, such as the National Man Suffrage Association in 1912. Their editorials and pamphlets emphasized that women needed the protection of men, were too emotional for voting, were subservient to men, and truly desired only to serve men. Comments Iowa legislators (all men) frequently made during the early twentieth century were similar to these:

> "A woman voting shows a 'lack of womanliness.'"
> "Women just need to get their husbands to the ballot box."
> "[Their] place is to be at home having babies."
> "Those suffragists just want to dominate submissive husbands."

Many anti-suffragist groups branded as evil the free-love movement that emphasized women's sexual freedom and use of birth control, despite multiple disclaimers by suffrage leaders that free love was not part of their movement. Anti-suffragists argued they were the defenders of the family and the nation by fighting to protect the sanctity of marriage and the welfare of children!

Businessmen often viewed enfranchised women as a threat to their political interests. Iowa newspaper editors and publishers in the late nineteenth and early twentieth centuries echoed these concerns in their arguments against women's suffrage. The arguments they put forth included:

1. The majority of women do not want the ballot. (No data exists to support this claim.)
2. The purity of the home would be compromised. (This thought derived from the rigid gender roles of the times.)
3. The local brewery industry may be harmed. (Owners were concerned that women would vote for temperance laws that would negatively impact breweries, particularly immigrant brewers who had no other sources of income.)

4. Suffragists were not responsible people or "good worthy women." (This misconception may be related to the very small number of suffragists who espoused free-love concepts.) (2)

In the introduction to his research on male opponents of women's suffrage, University of Northern Iowa History Professor Thomas Ryan notes the struggle for the vote was not just a "women against men battle" but "men against men" because men were the decision-makers in Congress and state legislatures. His data analysis concluded that male voting behavior, along with prevailing social attitudes about the roles of men and women, were factors in men's attitudes toward women's suffrage. His review of the defeated Iowa suffrage referendum in June 1916 identified ethnicity and religion in male voting behavior. "Dry counties, British-American counties, Protestant counties, and Republican counties returned the largest majorities for woman suffrage. Conversely, the proposal fared less well in wet counties, and in counties with the largest proportions of residents from continental Europe (especially Germany), Roman Catholic, and Democratic counties." Community size and rural or urban residency had no relationship to voting behavior. (3)

Another factor that isn't always discussed is that female leaders of the anti-suffrage national movement were not only well-to-do, but they were primarily urban, native-born, Republican, and Protestant. Most were already involved in philanthropy in their communities, as well as in social endeavors to better the lives of the poor. Therefore, these women could be labeled elitists, who saw universal suffrage as a threat to their own positions of privilege, their influence over their male family members, and their community connections and power. Even though Iowa was essentially rural, these same types of female anti-suffragists were active in the state, primarily in Des Moines and other large communities.

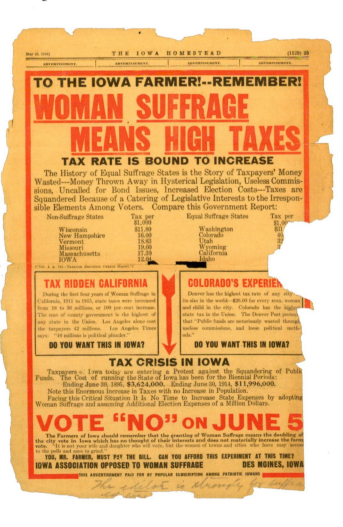

Typical advertising before the vote on the 1916 Iowa Woman Suffrage Amendment. Courtesy of State Historical Society of Iowa, May 25, 1916.

In 1913 and 1915, both houses of the Iowa General Assembly passed an amendment to the Iowa Constitution removing "male" from the voting section, thus enfranchising women. A statewide referendum on the issue was held June 5, 1916. It was defeated by 10,341 votes in what was described as a corrupt election (see Chapter 2 Appendix, Carrie Chapman Catt). The campaign for passage and its defeat in Iowa heightened national interest in moving forward with a federal constitutional amendment rather than the state-by-state approach organizers had been using.

The Final Campaign

A constitutional amendment for women's suffrage was first introduced in Congress by California Senator Aaron A. Sargent in 1878. He, then others, re-introduced it annually for forty-one years! Between 1878 and May 19, 1919, when Illinois Representative James R. Mann introduced the women's suffrage bill in Congress, fifteen state legislatures gave women unrestricted voting rights; twenty-eight states afforded rights to women to vote in presidential elections; and most other states granted varying degrees of local women's suffrage. Iowa granted women the right to vote on municipal and school bond issues in 1894. (4)

Two presidents supported suffrage on the road to the Nineteenth Amendment—Teddy Roosevelt and Woodrow Wilson. Former President Roosevelt's support for women's suffrage grew from his efforts to form a platform for the Progressive Party at its 1912 convention. He said, "A vote is like a rifle: Its usefulness depends upon the character of the user … I believe in suffrage for women in America because I think they are fit for it. I believe for women, as for men, more in the duty of fitting one's self to do well and wisely with the ballot than in the naked right to cast the ballot." (5) Support for women's suffrage ended up in the party's platform, though Mr. Roosevelt never saw it happen. He died five months before Congress passed the Nineteenth Amendment and sent it to the states for ratification.

After meeting with Alice Paul, who had organized a large suffrage parade on Pennsylvania Avenue in early March 1913, President Wilson was not moved to support women's suffrage. But by September 1918, as a result of U.S. center-stage involvement in World War I, he changed his mind and urged Congress to pass the Nineteenth Amendment. He told the Senate the people of the world "are looking to the great, powerful, famous democracy of the West to lead them to the new day for which they have so long waited; and they think … that democracy means that women shall play their part in affairs alongside men and upon an equal footing with them … without their counsellings [sic] we shall be only half wise." (6)

The U.S. House approved the amendment May 21, 1919, and the Senate followed on June 4. A number of states raced to be first to ratify the amendment, with Illinois winning out and ratifying it first, Wisconsin second, and Michigan third. Within the first four months, fourteen more states ratified—Kansas, New York, Ohio, Pennsylvania, Massachusetts, Texas, Iowa (the tenth state to ratify on July 2, 1919), Missouri, Arkansas, Nebraska, Montana, Minnesota, New Hampshire, and Utah—representing forty-seven percent of the goal of thirty-six states. (7)

The campaigns by state suffrage organizations continued, with assistance from the national organizers led by Carrie Chapman Catt. Tennessee would be the thirty-sixth state to ratify on August 18, 1920. Representative Harry T. Burn, a twenty-five-year-old freshman Republican legislator, lawyer, and president of the First National Bank & Trust in Rockwood, Tennessee, has his place in women's suffrage history, perhaps in large part due to his mother, Febb Ensminger Burn of Niota, Tennessee. She was a strong-willed farmer's widow who had followed the suffrage movement in four newspapers and dozens of magazines, in between chores of milking cows, churning butter, and cleaning, mending, and preparing meals for the family. Mrs. Burn said, "Suffrage has interested me for years. I like the suffrage militants as well as the others." She had just read a vitriolic speech against suffrage aimed to inspire her son's anti-suffrage constituents, so she felt she needed to communicate with him. "I sat down on [my] little chair on the front porch and penned a few lines to my son." (Mrs. Burn's letter was actually seven pages long.)

> Dear Son, … hurry and vote for suffrage and don't keep them in doubt. I noticed Chandlers' speech, it was very bitter. I've been waiting to see how you stood but have not seen anything yet … Don't forget to be a good boy and help Mrs. Catt and her 'Rats.' Is she the one that put 'rat' in ratification? Ha! No more from mama this time. With lots of love, Mama.

Mr. Burn faced the dilemma of representing his anti-suffrage constituents in the face of his own quiet support of women's suffrage. He wore a red rose in his lapel, a symbol of anti-suffrage. He wanted to delay a final decision until the next year's session, after his hoped-for re-election that fall. However, the motion to table the amendment in the House was defeated in a 48–48 tie. After the Tennessee Senate voted in support of the amendment, the Speaker of the House moved to reconsider the original motion. Mr. Burn, with Mama's letter in his breast pocket, hoped his vote would not be the one to decide the fate of the amendment. But it was. He "listened to Mama" and voted "aye," resulting in a 49–47 victory for women's suffrage. That sent the Nineteenth Amendment to Congress to become the law of the land on August 26, 1920.

Tennessee anti-suffragists quickly labeled Harry Burn a traitor. They accused him of taking $10,000 from a Jewish immigrant legislator to change his vote and accepting a bribe from Governor Albert H. Roberts' secretary. Neither accusation was true. His response in the *Tennessee House Journal* explained that his decision had been based on morality, justice, his mother, and the glory of the Republican Party. But the attacks from anti-suffragists continued. "When I went home for a weekend, I would generally keep a bodyguard around so that no one would attack me," Mr. Burn said. Suffrage opponents accosted his mother as well, demanding that she disavow her letter to her son, which she refused to do. Despite the efforts of anti-suffragists, Mr. Burn won re-election, though Governor Roberts, who also was a suffrage supporter, did not.

Mr. Burn held public office much of his adult life, serving four years in the Tennessee House and four years in the Tennessee Senate. He was a member of the Tennessee State Planning Commission for six years and a delegate for Roane County for three Tennessee Constitutional Conventions. Later in life, Mr. Burn stated: "I had always believed that women had an inherent right to vote. It was a logical attitude from my standpoint. My mother was a college woman, a student of national and international affairs who took an interest in all public issues. She could not vote, yet the tenant farmers on our farm, some of whom were illiterate, could vote. On that roll call, confronted with the fact that I was going to go on record for time and eternity on the merits of the question, I had to vote for ratification." (8)

It is worth noting that eight states waited many years to ratify the Nineteenth Amendment, though it was the law of the land. All were Southern states: Maryland, Virginia, Alabama, Florida, Georgia, Louisiana, North Carolina, and Mississippi, which did not vote to ratify until 1984.

The passage of the Nineteenth Amendment fully enfranchised twenty-seven million women, including approximately five hundred thousand African American women in states without voting barriers. Such barriers, primarily in states below the Mason-Dixon line, included literacy tests and poll taxes that barred many women of color, as well as white women, from voting for decades. In states with poll taxes (not prohibited until the ratification of the Twenty-fourth Amendment in 1924), disenfranchisement of women could be closer to home. Male heads of households would often pay their own poll tax to vote, but not the poll tax for their wives or daughters. Thirteen Southern states did not fully enfranchise African American women until the Voting Rights

"Ding" Darling cartoon from September 9, 1920. "We suppose the disintegration of the home and the defeminization of mother is liable to take place now most any minute." Permission granted by the University of Iowa Photo Archives and the "Ding" Darling Wildlife Society.

Act of 1965 passed. Other minority groups also had to wait to feel the impact of the Nineteenth Amendment. Native American women and men did not gain citizenship and the right to vote until 1924; Chinese American women and men not until 1943; and Japanese and other Asian American women and men not until 1952.

Mrs. Jens (Anna) Thuesen of Black Hawk County has been recognized as the first woman in Iowa, and perhaps in the United States, to vote after the passage of the Nineteenth Amendment. On August 27, 1920, Mrs. Thuesen and twenty-six other women cast their ballots in an election to establish a consolidated school district in parts of Black Hawk and Grundy counties.

Could it be, though, that Iowa women registered and voted before 1920? Historian Louise Noun found evidence of at least one such occurrence. After ratification of the Fourteenth Amendment in 1868, some in the legal profession, such as Francis Minor (see Chapter 4), interpreted "citizens" and "persons" to include women and urged women to register and vote.

Others, however, taunted women with "mock registrations." In spring 1871, the Clarinda Registry Board in jest added the names of all women older than twenty-one to the rolls of registered voters. The year before, ninety-two residents of Clarinda and nearby Taylor County had sent a petition to Congress urging women's suffrage, one of many petitions Congress received each year. That effort may have motivated the board's mock registrations.

When the board's prank was publicized, "several gentlemen 'got on their ear' about it and erased their wives' names. Several ladies got their precious backs up also and erased their own names." (9) But twenty-seven-year-old teacher Keziah (Kizzie) Anderson of Clarinda did not erase her name and showed up at the polls to vote in October 1871. Her father, William Anderson, and a family friend, Edwin Henshaw, were election judges and accepted her ballot (both Mr. Henshaw and Miss Anderson had signed the 1870 petition). (9) So, Miss Anderson may have been the first woman to vote in Iowa. Or, she was the first woman to commit voter fraud!

"Revised," a cartoon by Kenneth Russell Chamberlain, 1917. Image courtesy Library of Congress.

Chapter 4

Remember the Gentlemen ...

The Men who Supported Women's Suffrage

IN MARCH 1776, Abigail Adams wrote to her husband John, who was attending the Second Continental Congress in Philadelphia, reminding him "... do remember the ladies and be more generous and favorable to them ..."

John Adams did not follow his wife's advice if she was implying woman suffrage, but no history of the League of Women Voters of Iowa would be "generous" without honoring the men who supported suffrage. Many worked with women to pass the Nineteenth Amendment or supported the women in their lives who were involved in the movement. And through the years many men have backed the League's voter registration and education work, as well as legislation that League members worked to make law. Since 1973, the Iowa League has welcomed men as members (see Chapter 6).

An example of an early supporter of women's right to vote is Francis Minor (1820–1892), an attorney, women's rights advocate, and husband of suffragist Virginia Minor. He co-founded and served as the first president of the Woman Suffrage Association of Missouri. He argued in 1869 that because the Fourteenth Amendment made no reference to sex or gender, only "citizens" and "persons," it granted women the right to the ballot. When his wife attempted to vote and was refused, he filed a lawsuit against the registrar, with Mrs. Minor named as co-plaintiff. The lawsuit was filed in Mr. Minor's name because women could not legally sue on their own behalf. The case went all the way to the U.S. Supreme Court, with a unanimous decision against the Minors. Susan B. Anthony (see Chapter 2 Appendix) wrote about him upon his death: "No man has contributed to the woman suffrage movement so much valuable constitutional argument and proof as Mr. Minor." (1) He was inducted in the Hall of Famous Missourians in 2013.

A more local supporter of women's suffrage, but in a behind-the-scenes manner, was James A. Devitt of Oskaloosa. He secured childcare to ensure that his wife could continue her suffrage work. Pauline Devitt was vice president of the Iowa Equal Suffrage Association. It was her responsibility to prepare the county suffrage organizations for the October 1919 convention in Boone when the suffrage association would dissolve and form the Iowa League of Women Voters. Mrs. Devitt had three small children but needed to travel around the state, so her husband hired a practical nurse to care for the children. The nanny, who became known as Aunt Kate, looked after the children during the three years their mother was on the road periodically working with suffragists across Iowa. Soon, a popular saying arose in Iowa when a woman needed help with her children: "Well, you just need an Aunt Kate!" It could also have been said that many suffragists needed a considerate and practical husband like James Devitt!

National and Iowa Men's Suffrage Organizations

The Men's League for Woman Suffrage formally organized in New York in July 1910. The organization's charter members were prominent men. Oswald Garrison Villard, publisher of the *Nation* and the *New York Evening Post*, was the idea man. Max Eastman was a writer of literature, philosophy, and society, and the public face of the organization. John Dewey was a philosopher, psychologist, and education reformer. George Foster Peabody was a banker and philanthropist. Others included Hungarian-born Rabbi Stephen Wise and Charles Culp Burlingham, president of the New York Bar Association. From its beginnings through 1917, the founding membership of 150 represented a politically diverse group of men who shared a common interest in women's suffrage. The organization grew to twenty thousand members and had affiliates in thirty states, including Iowa.

The organization began with an invitation to Mr. Villard from suffrage leader Anna Howard Shaw (see Chapter 2 Appendix), then president of the National American Woman Suffrage Association (NAWSA), to speak at the 1908 suffrage convention in Buffalo, New York. Mr. Villard's mother, Fanny Garrison Villard, a supporter of women's suffrage and the daughter of abolitionist William Lloyd Garrison, had heard of the British Men's Suffrage Association. She urged her son to communicate with Miss Shaw about a men's suffrage organization to wield the electoral power of men. When Mr. Villard received the invitation, he responded to Miss Shaw that he was too busy to develop an elaborate speech for the event. Instead he asked if the organization would like him to assemble a group of one hundred influential men to support the cause in the form of a men's suffrage association. Miss Shaw and other suffrage leaders made a strategic decision and readily accepted Mr. Villard's offer. They subsequently benefitted from this alliance with powerful men who became very active supporters of the movement.

Many of the men who joined the Men's League may have done so to improve the heart of the polity, as well as the minds of women; tear down the Victorian era's sexual constraints; uphold the civilities of gender decorum; honor family connections to reform; and liberate all citizens from behavioral stereotypes. Joining the Men's League and taking a public stand on women's suffrage was not an easy task. Opponents of women's suffrage hurled derisive remarks at the one thousand men who marched in the 1912 New York City suffrage parade. Newspaper editors wrote abusive articles about the men and their efforts to support the movement. Johanna Neuman in 2017 concluded in her "Case for Mere Men" that "it took so much more courage for a man to come out for the women's suffrage parade than it did for a woman." (2)

Eileen Reynolds, in her 2017 post on the humility of men backing suffrage, describes male organizations' major efforts in support of the movement. Men first moved the argument from one of women's moral purity and female domesticity to the logic of democratic justice. Then, they "used their connections and political clout to advance the suffragist causes in spheres women couldn't otherwise have as easily reached. They argued in favor of women's suffrage in prestigious publications; lobbied political operatives to get the issue into party platforms and served on committees to get suffrage bills before legislatures; … and raised campaign funds." (3) And, when the Nineteenth Amendment became a reality, the organization and its members did not take credit away from women. In public statements they recognized the heroic action and hard, steady work of women and women's suffrage associations. Brooke Krueger called these well-organized and public supporters of women's suffrage "suffragents" in her award-winning book *The Suffragents: How Women Used Men to Get the Vote* (SUNY Press, 2017).

In Iowa a group of Des Moines men founded the Iowa Men's League for Woman Suffrage in 1916. Like the national organization, the Des Moines group consisted of a mix of professional men, including attorney John D. Dennison Jr., its first president. "In the final analysis, it will be the men who will have to decide the question of equal suffrage at the polls," Mr. Dennison said. "So we consider the matter a man's job as well as woman's and for that reason the men of the state are organizing to do their part in the campaign." When organizing other groups in the state, such as Perry in Dallas County, and Cedar Rapids, he remarked,

"Woman asks for the vote, not because she is a woman, but because she is an adult human being in a civilized society, and entitled to a voice in the affairs of state under whose laws she is holden, whose cause she serves, and whose burdens she helps." (4)

The formation of Iowa men's suffrage organizations rested in part on a foundation established by the Iowa Equal Suffrage Association (IESA). The association developed relationships with various groups across the state, primarily by giving speeches about suffrage to expose their audiences to the cause and hopefully "win over" some of them. Many of these potential suffrage supporters were prominent men and women, including mayors and other elected officials, members of the Federation of Women's Clubs or the Woman's Christian Temperance Union, journalists, and clergy. Mary Stafford, IESA president in 1911–12, spoke in Cherokee, Corydon, and Forest City to groups of men about the formation of a Men's League for Woman Suffrage in their communities. Some of the attendees at earlier IESA presentations may have later helped form Men's League groups.

Men's suffrage organizations offered advice to women's suffrage groups in Iowa, organized campaign events in collaboration with the IESA, and raised money for the cause. In 1917, they held a Valentine's Day Ball at the Cedar Rapids Hotel Montrose, with the main dining room turned into a ballroom adorned with red suffrage hearts. "Suffrage yellow" spring flowers greeted the guests, many of whom were prominent residents of the community. One of them donated the services of the Norman Ballheim Orchestra. The sponsoring organization used the profits from admissions that evening to cover IESA debts from the failed 1916 Iowa suffrage referendum.

A 1918 postcard designed to recruit Iowa men to the suffrage movement.

A probable member of the Iowa Men's League for Woman Suffrage was Harvey Ingham (1858–1949). Born of pioneer parents in Algona, he received a law degree from the State University of Iowa in 1881. Mr. Ingham was an editor of the *Algona Upper Des Moines* weekly newspaper for twenty years and served as postmaster for four years. He served a six-year term on the Iowa Board of Education. In 1903, he began a long-term partnership with Gardner Cowles, who owned the *Des Moines Register and Leader*, which later became the *Des Moines Register*. The newspaper's motto: "The newspaper Iowa depends upon." It was a Pulitzer Award-winning, independent paper with a circulation of 350,000 in 1927. A forty-year editor, Mr. Ingham gave his reporters a directive: "Tell the truth and let the chips fall where they may." He was a progressive Republican who supported fellow Republican Teddy Roosevelt's efforts to rein in trusts, as well as Democrat Woodrow Wilson's attempt to join the League of Nations, stating: "The wisest nationalism the American citizen will ever show will be the nationalism that is international." (5)

Harvey Ingham near the beginning of his editorial career. State Historical Society, Des Moines.

Mr. Ingham was "a staunch champion of women's suffrage" who spoke many times at League of Women Voters functions. In her seminal work on the Iowa suffrage movement, Louise Noun described him as "one of the great liberal editors of the state." (6) She included several of his quotations: "… [I] favor 'youthful minds in old bodies …'" "every extension of liberty has vindicated itself," "the more rights people have the more responsibilities they assume," and "no nation ever went upon the rocks because of liberty." (7)

Early in his career, Mr. Ingham spoke out and worked against racism. He was heavily involved in the educational programs of the Des Moines chapter of the NAACP. Drake University honored his civic involvement and the impact of his editorial career with the construction of the Harvey Ingham Science Building, dedicated in 1949 shortly before his death. The building recently was remodeled and remains in use today.

CATHOLIC PRELATE ENDORSES SUFFRAGE FOR IOWA WOMEN

BISHOP AUSTIN DOWLING
Of Des Moines

I, for one, contemplate the prospect of equal suffrage in Iowa with satisfaction, and unless all signs fail there is no doubt the verdict of the people will at last give it to women.

No vote, no influence, is almost an axiom in present politics. You get nothing unless you have influence; you have no influence unless you can vote.

Many of our clergy have been in favor of equal suffrage. I am told that the late Archbishop Reardon, of San Francisco, issued a pastoral to encourage women to vote. Archbishop Delaney, of Hobart, in Tasmania, in a letter, flouts the criticism of woman suffrage and wrote in the London Tablet, January 18, 1913, "I can speak for our Tasmanian women, both Catholic and Protestant, that to my knowledge, and I am in a position to know, not one has ever forgotten the dignity of her sex or her self-respect, or done any of the things that sometimes befall men on such occasions as political elections."

Many prominent and influential members of the hierarchy, like late Cardinals Vaughn and Moran, and, I believe, all of the Bishops of Australia and some of our own country, are among the outspoken and confirmed upholders of Votes for Women. It is sure that no candidate has any chance of purchasing a woman's vote at the drink shop.

Men have so long spoken of the Fatherland, that they forget that under another personification it may very properly be spoken of as the Mother country, the government of which calls quite as much for the motherly qualities of women as for the administrative and deliberative powers of man.

IOWA EQUAL SUFFRAGE ASSOCIATION
FLEMING BUILDING 25 **DES MOINES, IOWA**

Support for women's suffrage was found among clergy as well. Bishop Austin Dowling (1868–1930) was born in New York and ordained in 1891. In 1912, he was appointed bishop of Des Moines, where he established the Des Moines Catholic College in 1918 (now Dowling Catholic High School). He wrote a pamphlet for the Iowa Equal Suffrage Association in support of women voting. Because of this advocacy, he may well have been a colleague of Mr. Ingham. In 1919, Bishop Dowling moved to St. Paul, Minnesota, to become archbishop. He was known as "a man who was by taste, habit, and profession a historian; he could not set about finding solutions to problems facing him until he examined those problems in the light of the past." (8)

LOGIC FOR THE BUSINESS MAN

Women **have proved** their **business sense**, their **honesty**, their **ability** in thousands and thousands of business positions—as owners, managers, and in office work.

How many women cashiers have you known to run off with their employers' money?

Aren't **the women** in your office as intelligent, **as steady** and as **reliable** as the men?

Isn't it "good business" in your line of work to build up an **experienced, honest, loyal** force of experts?

In the **great business** of legislating for women and children wouldn't it be "good business" to get the help and vote of **women** who are **experts** in these needs?

As **85 per cent** of those who buy are women, wouldn't it be "good business" to give women an interest in tariff legislation and in conditions that affect the making and the sale of goods?

Would any business man **endure being bound** by contracts to which he was not a party? Isn't that what every woman is obliged to do who is **taxed without representation?**

Do you have to take much time away from your business to prepare for voting, or to vote?

Because you have the ballot, does it make you want to **run for office**, or **neglect your** duties or **your home?**

You do not deny to women stockholders **the right to protect** their interests by a vote.

PLEASE BE LOGICAL.

VOTE for the WOMAN SUFFRAGE AMENDMENT, JUNE 5

Iowa Equal Suffrage Association

Fleming Building, Des Moines, Iowa

The Des Moines Printing Company

324.3

From the collections of the State Historical Society, Des Moines.

Other Iowa Male Supporters of Women's Suffrage

The support of countless other men was instrumental in helping women gain the right to vote. Those men include:

- Male legislators who crafted and supported the Iowa constitutional amendment for universal suffrage that was defeated at the polls in June 1916;
- Men who voted for ratification of the Nineteenth Amendment on July 2, 1919; and
- Male legislators who voted in 1922 to remove the word "man" from the requirements to serve in the House of Representatives, and by implication, the Senate. The state constitutional amendment that effected this change was ratified in 1926. This action opened the doors for the first female member of the Iowa Legislature, Carolyn Campbell Pendray of Maquoketa (see Biographies Appendix).

For the interested reader: Additional male supporters of the suffrage movement are contained in Chapter 4 Appendix.

Campaign button from the Men's League For Women's Suffrage

Chapter 5

From Victory to the Informed Voter ...

The Formation of the
National League of Women Voters

WITH PASSAGE OF the Nineteenth Amendment imminent, suffrage activists gathered at a Jubilee Convention in St. Louis on March 24, 1919, to celebrate the fiftieth anniversary of the suffrage organization that became the National American Woman Suffrage Association (NAWSA), as well as the suffrage victories in a steadily expanding list of states. Carrie Chapman Catt used this event to organize the successor organization of NAWSA into what became known as the National League of Women Voters. The aim of this soon-to-be independent organization was educating all women—not just members of the organization—to actively participate in government when universal suffrage was obtained.

Formal organization of this successor group occurred February 14, 1920, at the Victory Convention in Chicago. NAWSA was dissolved and the first League of Women Voters convention officially began with seven hundred women attending. Mrs. Catt indicated that "the object of the organization was not to seek power in organizing ... but to foster education in citizenship and to support improved legislation." (1) To do the latter, the organization would be nonpartisan, supporting no candidates or political parties. Instead, the League's involvement in the political arena would focus on passing needed legislation based on thorough studies by League members, resulting in position statements to trigger action. Many in the field of political science at the time lauded this nonpartisanship as an innovative response to complicated issues needing government action. In fact, it probably has been "the key to the League's longevity" across the decades, according to Naomi Black, professor emerita in the Department of Politics at York University. (2)

47

THE LEAGUE!
"I, TOO, AM NON-PARTISAN, BUT NOT BLIND."

* Reprinted with permission of LWVUS.

Citizenship Schools and Beyond

Along with work on national and perhaps state legislation, Mrs. Catt had "always envisioned that organized suffragists would continue working for the liberation of women and for honest, responsive government once they had the vital tool of the vote. From the time she first became active in the suffrage movement she was appalled at how little women knew of the most elementary rules of parliamentary procedure, let alone of how a bill became an act [law]." (3) Mrs. Catt began a political science course in 1897 for her suffrage campaign workers. Women attended intermittently during the remaining twenty years of the suffrage movement. This course grew into the National League's Citizenship Schools. The program was established in 1920 as a priority activity for all Leagues and was instituted by League members across the United States. Mrs. Catt's ideal study curriculum included:

- Preamble to the U.S. Constitution;
- Local election laws;
- Practical demonstration of voting to build confidence and prepare women to become election officials;
- Powers of and election procedures for the executive branch;
- Civil government, including the duties of local, county, and state officials;
- Legislative bodies and how laws are made;

- How to change or get the law you want—the beginnings of the study and action processes of the League; and
- Money in politics—Mrs. Catt was ahead of her time!

These issues are the main components of civics curricula presented by teachers in our social studies classrooms across the nation today and are part of the many current activities that local Leagues use to educate community members about the workings of government. (See Citizenship Appendix)

"Ding" Darling cartoon from 1920. "The Advent of Women Voters." Permission granted by the University of Iowa Photo Archives and the "Ding" Darling Wildlife Society.

Early League Structure and Action (1920–1940s)

Based on the organizational structure of its predecessor, the National American Woman Suffrage Association, League leaders organized nationally, with state and local affiliates identified by congressional districts. Due to the methodology of the former NAWSA and the infancy of the League organization, leaders made top-down decisions about legislative action and management for many years. Initially, National League Board members were designated as "field officers." They offered considerable support and training on principles and procedures to state and local affiliates forming across the country. By 1924, 346 Leagues had been organized in 433 congressional districts.

With the recent end of World War I and the establishment of the League of Nations, the National League of Women Voters chose to focus on peacekeeping initiatives along with citizenship and voter education. The group also pushed for reforms primarily impacting women, such as equal opportunity in government and industry, and minimum wages. (4) The League set forth the following priorities during the first decade of its existence:

- Education, in the form of federal aid to address illiteracy, the support of compulsory education laws in states, and lobbying for increases in teachers' salaries;
- Public health, including the prevention of venereal diseases and public education in sexual hygiene—a definite example that the League has always been "ahead of the times";
- The home, in the form of vocational training in home economics and instruction on postwar realities for farm production, i.e. equalizing prices farmers received for their crops with costs paid for goods, along with the elimination of unfair competition and price controls for the necessities of life; and
- Child welfare, such as the prohibition of child labor and protection of infant life through a federal program for maternity and infant care to address the high maternal and infant death rates.

The latter program became the Sheppard-Towner Maternity and Infancy Act that passed November 23, 1921. It was the League's first effective use of grassroots organizing as a coalition with other organizations. Historians acknowledge the act was a landmark in the development of social welfare programs in the United States. It was the first major legislation that passed after the Nineteenth Amendment.

The 1930s. This decade found the League, like so many organizations and individuals, barely surviving the Depression. Membership fell from one hundred thousand in 1924 to forty-four thousand in 1934. A good outcome was that League members began to meet in small groups in their neighborhoods to discuss local issues, as well as threats to democracy. This local activity awakened the National League to the realization that more attention needed to be placed on individual Leagues' local

"Ding" Darling cartoon from June 24, 1922. "Rearranging Pa's Things for Him; Mere Man: If this thing keeps up, I won't know where to find a doggone thing." Permission granted by the University of Iowa Photo Archives and the "Ding" Darling Wildlife Society.

and state issues. The League still worked at the national level for the enactment of the Social Security and the Food and Drug Acts in this decade, as well as legislation in 1938 and 1940 that moved hundreds of federal jobs from the spoils system to a civil service system. To galvanize citizens to action in this effort, they used the campaign slogan "Find the Man for the Job, Not the Job for the Man" in newspapers and flyers. The League also began its involvement in environmental concerns with its support of the Tennessee Valley Authority, which passed in 1933.

The 1940s. The League supported the United Nations, the World Bank, and the International Monetary Fund, all part of the aftermath of World War II. During the 1944 National League Convention, amid pressure from state and local delegates, League leaders began the needed step of restructuring the League into national, state, and local units. That meant membership at the local level would be reflected as membership in the state and national League. National League leaders began communicating directly with state and local League presidents and boards of directors. Education for state and local Leagues to conduct studies, use the consensus method to form positions, and take action began in earnest. These changes transformed the League from a top-down organization to a tri-level organization where studies could be performed at the national, state, or local level. All local Leagues could participate in national and state studies and help reach consensus on resulting positions. In addition, local Leagues could undertake their own studies with the League study-consensus-position procedure, or a local League could use an already established state or national position for its action on a local issue. At the 1946 convention, the name of the organization was changed to the League of Women Voters of the United States.

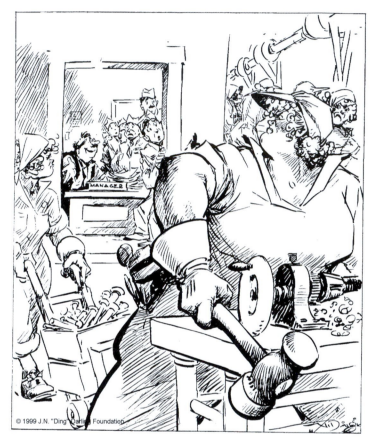

"Ding" Darling cartoon from July 29, 1947. "Shouldn't we add accident and health insurance to that job guarantee." Permission granted by the University of Iowa Photo Archives and the "Ding" Darling Wildlife Society.

The League after Restructure (1950s to Present)

The 1950s. In the post-World War II era, the National League created an Education Fund that could receive tax-deductible contributions for educational projects at all three levels of the League. The National League also established the *Voter* newsletter, which went to organizations and contributors, as well as members. In addition, the League provided advocacy skills training for League members, which laid the groundwork for participation in the civil rights and feminist movements in the 1960s and 1970s.

The 1960s. The League reached a high point in membership in the 1960s, with nearly 157,000 members nationwide. Apportionment was a national priority, and here in Iowa as well, along with presidential suffrage for Washington, D.C., residents. The League also was one of the first organizations in the United States to call for normalization of relations with China. The League applauded the 1961 creation of the Presidential Commission on the Status of Women and supported the 1963 Equal Pay Act, which the League had lobbied for since 1945. The League also supported the sex discrimination portion of Title VII of the Civil Rights Act in 1964. Many of us today wonder if these laws have been adequately enforced.

The 1970s. Along with allowing men to be full voting members of the League in the 1970s, the organization developed positions on water, air, waste management, land use, and energy. These positions have been used repeatedly in lobbying efforts by the Iowa League and other state Leagues, as well as local Leagues across the country. The League also continued its support of the United Nations and its programs. In 1976, the League sponsored the first televised presidential debates since 1960, winning an Emmy Award for Outstanding Achievement in Broadcast Journalism, along with praise from James Reston of the *New York Times*. He rated the League as a clear winner for getting the candidates together on the national stage for a true comparison of their views. The League also embraced civil and human rights by studying poverty, employment discrimination, and inequity in education. These issues continue to be relevant fifty years later.

"We put laws on the books; turn rights into realities; register millions to vote; and keep politics a process for the people."
—League of Women Voters membership campaign slogan for 1982–1983

The 1980s. During this decade, the League continued to sponsor presidential debates—in 1980 and 1984—until the political parties announced their future sponsorship of debates with the creation of the Commission on Presidential Debates. The League also was very active in support of the Voting Rights Act of 1982, as well as the historic Tax Reform Act of 1986. In 1983, the League adopted its current position on public policy on reproductive choice based on the constitutional right to privacy. It also underwrote 150 debates among congressional candidates on national security issues. In addition, the League was in the forefront of lobbying for ratification of the Intermediate-Range Nuclear Forces Treaty (INF) in 1988. The League also reaffirmed its commitment to lowering poverty and reforming the welfare system, and it began work on campaign finance reform to curb the influence of special interest groups—an issue the League continues to work on.

The 1990s. The League's achievements in this decade began with passage of the National Voter Registration Act, known as the "Motor Voter Bill." It became law in 1993 after a previous presidential veto.

This legislation enabled thousands of citizens to register to vote at state-run motor vehicle agencies, as well as by mail and at government offices that serve the public. This is an example of how states like Iowa benefitted from the League's lobbying efforts on issues with national impact. President Bill Clinton praised the League and other supporters of the bill, calling them "fighters for freedom" in their continued efforts to expand American democracy.

The 2000s. To begin the new century, the League worked to pass the Help America Vote Act and the Bipartisan Campaign Finance Reform Act, both adopted in 2002, and pushed for the renewal of the Voting Rights Act. The League filed amicus briefs with the Supreme Court on issues of campaign finance reform, racial bias in jury selection, and Title IX. In congressional legislative work, the League focused on re-districting, civil liberties, campaign finance reform, voting rights for Washington, D.C., residents, election administration reform and ethics, and lobbying reform—all under LWVUS's "Democracy Agenda."

The 2010s. In 2011, the League led the "Power the Vote" campaign, opposing measures to restrict access to voting that primarily affected minorities, the elderly, students, and rural residents. In 2014, the League began a study of the "Structures of Democracy" to review money in politics, redistricting, and the constitutional amendment process. In 2017, the League filed an amicus brief in the U.S. Supreme Court case of Gill v. Whitford, arguing that partisan gerrymandering violates the First Amendment and the equal protection clause of the Fourteenth Amendment. In 2018, the Supreme Court remanded the case back to the district court for further review, the result of the 5–4 decision that partisan gerrymandering claims are nonjusticable.

Since its beginning, the LWVUS has positively impacted the lives of Americans by working for legislation affecting children and families, education, the environment, good government, health care, and human rights, as well as by striving to protect the right to vote and providing information necessary to exercise that right, which is the foundation of a democracy. As President Harry Truman stated, "No government is perfect. One of the chief virtues of a democracy, however, is that its defects are always visible and under democratic processes can be pointed out and corrected." The League has been helping to "point out and correct" those defects for one hundred years despite founder Carrie Chapman Catt's prediction that "the education of women in politics could be accomplished quickly, and after a few years the League would disband ... although some people who were in the spirit of the new movement may discover it is an organization worth perpetuating." (5) Let's hope the League "perpetuates" for another one hundred years!

In that vein, the LWVUS governing board is made up of experienced individuals committed to meeting the current challenges. They know an organization such as the League needs to be looking ten to twenty years into the future to survive, not the five years Mrs. Catt thought was sufficient to "being ahead of the game." The more than seven hundred state and local Leagues in all fifty states exhibit vast differences that the national League needs to consider when making policies and providing assistance. Along with monitoring action in Congress and designing and producing voter education materials—just a couple of the myriad tasks of the LWVUS—the organization is fully committed to diversity, equity, and inclusion in principle and in practice. To that end, the group launched a training program for all Leagues, explaining how to achieve these goals in their individual settings. The current LWVUS Board also emphasizes increased use of technology, from Zoom meetings to social media posts. The national League has identified fostering communication among local Leagues as a need and a priority. That mirrors a goal of LWVUS Board member Dr. Deb Turner, former Iowa League co-president (2015–16), who has a mantra: "Sharing information moves an organization ahead by leaps and bounds." And lastly, the board recognizes our aging membership and the need to revitalize with younger individuals who share an interest in government decision-making at all levels—local, state, and national—and who come with needed skills, strengths, and energy. To that end, a new generation of staff at the Washington, D.C., League office is heading up a "get 'em young and train 'em up" initiative!

Deborah Turner, MD, JD, (right) was elected League of Women Voters of the United States President in June 2020. She is the first former LWVIA President to hold the office, and the second woman of color to do so. (Photo from Turner's 2013 Iowa Women's Hall of Fame induction ceremony with Phyllis Peters, Director of the Iowa Department of Human Rights.)

League's VIP Process

To work for new laws and changes in laws, a national organization needs a structure to "get 'er done." The League has developed and practiced the following processes to reach that goal:

V = Verify a need or problem in specific terms, preferably, as Mrs. Catt recommended, years ahead of others:

> [Mrs. Catt] wanted the League to lead the way, to be ahead of the political parties by at least five years. Traveling in the rear of the procession was too dusty and dirty, in the middle it was too crowded, only in the lead was the air clean and bracing. (6)

I = Investigate the issue from a variety of resources, preferably data-based. This practice originated in the nineteenth century with social reformers working for change in their communities:

> Former League President Dr. Gail Quinn (1999–2001) of Ottumwa noted, "… in League work I learned how to examine an issue from both sides, which is a different approach than one uses as a physician; and I learned to work with different groups of people with differing perspectives and thus opinions … which served me well in League and in my community."

P = Plan. Develop a plan of action, based on member discussion of the study results and the consensus* reached on a League position, and persist in the work needed to impact decision-makers for change—in League lingo, study and action. (See Chapter 9 for examples of local Leagues' study and action) [*The consensus process may have originated with Quaker suffragists and their process of decision-making within their communities.]

Why can this League process be labeled with the contemporary acronym VIP (Very Important Process)? League founders were far ahead of their time to develop a decision-making process and action plan in the real world. Recent scholarly investigation and research have validated the methods that the League has used to study problems and work for change.

Verify and state specifically: The League process for identifying a problem is similar to the guidance Iowan William Edwards Deming developed in the 1950s. While in Japan to assist in the rebuilding of that nation's industries after World War II, Mr. Deming developed the Total

Quality Management process. Mr. Deming advised seeking information about a problem from those closest to it, i.e. going to the source, as well as dealing with one aspect of a problem at a time. He coupled that with Mahatma Gandhi's guidance: "If you want people to listen to you, you have to listen to them; if you hope people will change, you have to know how they live; and if you want people to see you, you have to sit down with them eye-to-eye." (7) Mr. Deming's process provides a good model for accurately identifying a need or problem from those who are most knowledgeable and who will probably be part of the solution.

Variety of resources: Mr. Deming also said, "There is no substitute for knowledge." (8) And true knowledge is derived from a wealth of information, drawn from different sources, which has been organized and synthesized for meaning. Errors in human judgment will negatively impact sources of information, whether written or spoken. Errors stem from faulty information provided to the reporter, incorrectly applied logic of the reporter, and/or biased acquisition of the information by the reporter. Having information from many sources tends to level out the negative impact of individuals' judgment errors, again an approach that is foundational to the League's study process.

Data-based: Mr. Deming said, "In God we trust, all others must bring data." (9) Data, defined as measurements with reliable instruments, tabulations, and statistics, is not easily contaminated by human bias. Bias can take two forms: implicit, which is unknown to the person and others, though it impacts thinking and responses; and explicit, which is obvious to self or others. Because data is less prone to these biases, it is a far more reliable source of information than opinion or casual observation. That's why the League's approach centers on gathering data and not opinion about an issue or problem. (Visit https://implicit.harvard.edu/implicit/takeatest.html to check out your own implicit biases with one or more of fourteen Implicit Association Tests, on topics such as race, age, and weight. Or read Dolly Chugh's book, *The Person You Mean to Be: How Good People Fight Bias*. [Harper Collins Publishers, 2018.])

Also, memories are affected by temporal, negative, and vividness effects—meaning how near or far away an event happened, if we perceived the event as negative, and if it was intense or emotional in some way. In addition, we can be impacted by confirmation bias, a tendency to embrace information that supports our own beliefs and reject information that contradicts them. And there is a consensus effect, in which we think everyone feels the same way about something as we do. Suffrage leaders and League founders recognized these normal human tendencies that can distort memories and bias opinions years before scientific theories were posited. Leaguers have always "counted stuff" from lots of sources in order to clarify an issue or problem, which leads to better problem-solving, and worked with an awareness of the negative impact of bias.

Consensus: Reviewing all pertinent information, discussing it, and coming to an agreement on a publicly stated position builds ownership of an issue and an individual commitment to support action. Former LWVIA President Abbi Swanson (1993–95), whose grandmother was a founding member of the first League of Women Voters of Chicago and whose mother was active in the League well into her 70s, shared, "The consensus process of the League, taking data and looking at it in varying ways in order to come to a decision or a statement of belief, has helped my professional work with clients."

Persistence: The founders of the League had been working for women's suffrage for many years, so they were quite knowledgeable of how long it takes for change to occur and why a campaign needs to persist. Since that time, scholars have researched why people resist change and identified the six most common reasons:

1. Fear of the unknown.
2. Fear of making a mistake.
3. Fear of lacking needed competence.
4. Losing control of a situation.
5. Unwillingness to do the work that change may require.
6. Fear of negative ramifications, such as job loss, that the change may present.

Also, change is easiest when those involved share a high level of trust. It is hard to build trust among the members of a large group, such as decision-makers in government who come from varying backgrounds, experiences, and even cultures. Specialists in organizational development and change report that in institutions such as schools or corporations, even among people who are familiar with each other, major changes in operation or philosophies can take up to seven years to master. That's the case even with good internal leadership, appropriate expectations at various stages of the change, and support from external facilitators. It's no wonder it takes so long for elected and appointed officials in local, state, and national governments, who may be working in environments that lack the trust level of families or communities, to get things done. Also, individual government officials may not remain in their positions long enough for significant change to occur. When discussing leadership, President Dwight D. Eisenhower summarized the need to work with a variety of individuals with different perspectives and goals: "It is persuasion—and conciliation—and education—and patience. It is long, slow, and tough work." (10)

And sociology scholars would caution those working for change that it can take an entire generation of evolution to develop new ways of thinking or for conditions to emerge in a society that force change, such as the impact of ecological, technological, and economic realities. Thus, Leaguers "soldier on, acting on the staunch belief that along with the power of the vote and with the commitment to social change, we can build a better nation, provide for the common welfare, and help humanity upward." (11)

All the League of Women Voters of the United States public policy positions established after study and consensus, and used for lobbying at the national, state, and local levels, can be found at www.lwv.org/impact-issues.

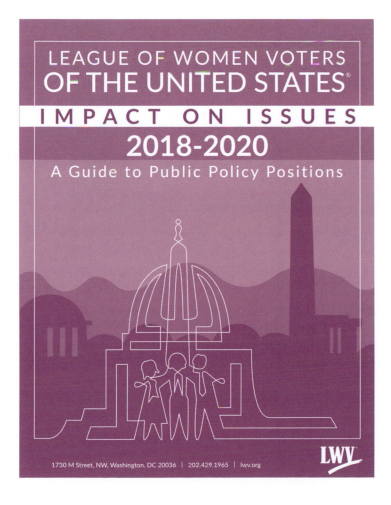

Cover of the LWVUS *Impact on Issues, 2018–2020.*

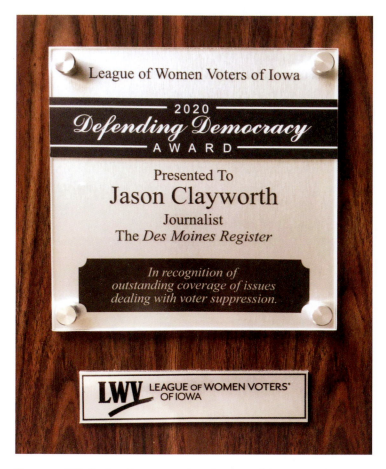

First annual Defending Democracy Award presented June 2020 to Jason Clayworth, investigative reporter for the *Des Moines Register* for his investigation of and reporting on Iowa's flawed felon database. His work revealed that some Iowans have been disqualified as legitimate voters. The Office of the Secretary of State is now following a six-step verification process for identifying felons who have completed their incarceration and removing non-felons from the voter database.

Chapter 6

From Citizenship Schools to Environmental Activism ...

The League of Women Voters of Iowa

The First Decade of the Iowa League

The Iowa League of Women Voters, the original name of the state League, was one of the first Leagues in the nation because Iowa was the home state of suffrage leader Carrie Chapman Catt. And because of Mrs. Catt's presence, Iowa had several well-organized and hard-working suffrage groups. The Iowa League's formation predated that of the National League by four months, forming October 2, 1919, at the Hotel Holst (see Glossary Appendix) in Boone, when the Iowa Equal Suffrage Association disbanded.

Des Moines social worker Flora Dunlap was the first president (1919–20) of the Iowa League (see Chapter 2 Appendix). Previously, she had been president of the Iowa Equal Suffrage Association for three years (1913–16). Her duties primarily consisted of traveling the state by car to support suffrage groups. A *Des Moines Register* article carried the following Iowa League convention report: "Club members, who for years have been using their indirect influence for the passage of better road laws, better laws for women and children, better housing, and better hours of labor for women, are now ready to help create and to better fit themselves for the task, and are embodying within their club schedule for study of such topics as will fit them for better citizenship." (1)

Early Iowa Leagues were organized on a countywide basis, as suffrage groups had been. Some of the first Leagues in the 1920s, after the March 1920 formation of the Iowa City League*, included Hamilton, Humboldt, Linn*, Mahaska in April, Marshall, Polk*, Pocahontas, Scott, Wapello*, and Woodbury* (the asterisk denotes Leagues still in existence, although perhaps with different names). As the years passed, more and more local Leagues formed. At one time, forty-five Leagues existed (see Chapter 10). For the first three years, a regional director assigned by the National League made frequent visits to Iowa. The goal was to strengthen the operation of the Iowa League Board of Directors as they strove to form and serve local Leagues, as well as act on the national program.

The first Iowa convention was September 23, 1920, right after the Nineteenth Amendment was ratified. Grace Brown became the League's second president, serving for one year. One-year terms remained a common practice for four more presidents until bylaws changed to allow two-year terms. Dues for members were minimal in the beginning. Major financing for League activities came from munificent contributions of men and women who believed in the value of educating women for effective citizenship. One such benefactor was Rose Frankel Rosenfeld, a close friend of Flora Dunlap and the mother of Louise Noun. This type of League financing dwindled in subsequent decades, and higher member dues needed to be assessed. A song lyric by an unidentified local Leaguer or perhaps two or more working together, which is the League way, was adapted from the popular 1965 song "What the World Needs Now is Love." (2) It reflects the financial situation of the Iowa League and its local Leagues for most of our history:

> What our League needs now is money, sweet money,
> It's the only thing that there's just too little of,
> What our League needs now is money, more money …
> No, not just from us, but from everyone!
> Lord, we don't need another item—there are items and
>   projects enough to do.
> There are meetings and papers enough to read—enough to last
>   'til the end of time!
> What our League needs now is money, sweet money,
> It's the only thing that there's just too little of,
> What our League needs now is money, more money …
> No, not just from us, but from everyone!
> Lord, we need those informed voters—there are people and
>   issues on which to vote!
> There are pamphlets and booklets we need to buy—enough to
>   last 'til the end of time!
> What our League needs now is money, sweet money,
> It's the only thing that there's just too little of,
> What our League needs now is money, more money …
> No, not just from some, but from everyone …
> So we can help not just us, but everyone!

During the first League convention, members discovered outgoing President Dunlap did not have a gavel to use when presiding over the convention. A Floyd County League member secured part of a cedar tree from Carrie Chapman Catt's girlhood home and had two gavels made—one for the Iowa League president's use and one for Mrs. Catt as a tribute gift. At that convention, a League Memorial Association was established to work on a fitting Iowa suffrage memorial. It was installed and dedicated by Carrie Chapman Catt in 1936. The bronze panel in bas relief was placed on the north wall of the first-floor rotunda in the Iowa Capitol. It features a pioneer and modern suffrage woman, with the suffrage torch passed from the older to the younger woman, symbolizing the need to carry on future reforms.

Iowa Suffrage Memorial bas relief, Iowa State Capitol, created by Iowa sculptor Nellie Verne Walker. State Historical Society of Iowa, Des Moines.

Because of the infancy of the organization and the importance of preparing women for informed voting, the National League Board of Directors mandated state and local Leagues topics of study and action—called the program. In Iowa, emphasis also was placed on election laws, how to complete a ballot, candidate information for voters, and political party operations and policies. The latter topic soon was dropped because of problems remaining nonpartisan on issues if League members became too involved in a political party.

In fact, Clear Lake resident and former Iowa League President Hazel Knutson's husband, Clarence, was a member of the Iowa House of Representatives from 1923 to 1929, during her League presidency (1926–28). This was a violation of the rules of a purportedly nonpartisan organization. The situation, also apparent in other states as Leagues were learning to be nonpartisan, led the National League to establish definite limitations on members' political activity while serving on a board at any level—national, state, and local (see Glossary Appendix).

Citizenship Schools were plentiful across Iowa and reportedly drew large numbers of individuals who wanted to learn more about the workings of government (see Chapter 5). The first such school was held in February 1920 in Iowa City, with 250 women in attendance. The next month, Des Moines held an extensive three-day program that included speakers on topics including municipal government, state boards and commissions, and courts and their jurisdiction. The state League worked with women's clubs and Parent Teacher Associations in communities that did not have a local League to organize these schools. Iowa State University Extension also was an early collaborator with the League in conducting Citizenship Schools. State board minutes in 1923 noted election officials were a primary target for these schools. The League also collaborated early on with a social workers organization, working with the group in the 1920s to establish mental hygiene (early term for mental health) clinics in various Iowa communities.

It became evident very quickly to Iowa League members, who were quite knowledgeable of their communities and state, that the Iowa Constitution needed amending to eliminate provisions that discriminated against the legal and economic rights of women. In addition, many new or improved laws were needed in the following areas: providing equal wages for equal work; improving working conditions for women in industry; improving the care, health, welfare, and education of children; making government more efficient at all levels; and expanding international cooperation for the prevention of future wars. This latter issue became a study item sent down from the National League. Thus, in addition to state issues for improving the quality of life for Iowans, many local Leagues spent time studying the causes and cures of war, adherence to the World Court, and the League of Nations. Florence Prather Pierce of Des Moines, Iowa League president from 1921 to 1922, commented about the early work of the League, "… [our efforts] took the League from the society pages to the editorial page."

A November 23, 1921, opinion piece in the *Des Moines Tribune* titled "A Splendid Movement" contained glowing words about the new Iowa League of Women Voters, "… [it] has impressed itself in a short year or two upon the public as one of the really worthwhile movements in American politics. Wholly non-partisan and made up of the leaders of all of the political movements, it aims to center on the things which everybody ought to be interested in and know about. Its work is constructive … the women who are part of it are bound to hear about public affairs, not as republicans [sic] or democrats [sic], but as citizens … it would be fortunate if men could meet in such a league, not as [party members] but as citizens, and consider the great national problems once in a while from that angle … the women are likely to be the real leaders of public opinion in the next few years if they work along the lines they are now on. A serious consideration of great problems in the spirit of good citizenship is bound to materially affect our political alignments, and to bring more intelligence into our party programs."

A League Operating Principle: Be "Ahead of the Game"

> "If the League of Women Voters hasn't the vision to see what is coming and what ought to come, and be five years ahead … I doubt if it is worth the trouble to go on."—Carrie Chapman Catt in an address to the Congress of the League of Women Voters on February 14, 1920. (3)

An early directive from the founder of the League was to be "ahead of the game," i.e. identify and begin to address problems and issues before others are fully aware. In other words, always be thinking ahead. Iowa League President Mary Dresser's speech at the fiftieth State Convention in 1969 addressed this topic. The speech, titled "The Past is Prologue," shared guidance on this approach for creating change from social scientist John Gardner (1912–2002). "An organization whose maturing consists simply of acquiring more firmly established ways of doing things is headed for the graveyard—even if it learns to do these things with greater and greater skill. … In the ever-renewing organization, what matures is a system or framework within which continuous innovation, renewal, and rebirth can occur." (4)

Here are some examples of the Iowa League's "thinking ahead and moving forward," which offered continuous renewal for the organization while providing decision-makers information for needed change or innovation:

- In the 1930s, the League not only supported low-cost public housing, but also lobbied for a new formula of state aid to public schools. Members also informed the public about issues of the day via a monthly WSUI radio broadcast from the League office in Iowa City.
- The 1940s found the League distributing a pamphlet statewide, "Government and our Minorities," with information about ways the government could equalize opportunities for minority groups and women—still an issue today.
- A discussion of reapportionment began in the 1950s. The League wanted impartial legislative and congressional districts to protect Iowans' right to fair representation. Many legislators were not familiar with the issue and needed education and information, as well as methods to form districts in a non-

partisan manner to counter gerrymandering. Former Iowa House member Gladys Shand Nelson (1951–57) of Newton, also a former LWVIA president (1937–39), commented at the thirty-fifth League anniversary that "over the years the League has done a tremendous job molding public opinion and sponsoring worthwhile legislation, far greater than its [member] numbers would indicate."

- At that same celebration, Anna Louise Strong of Grinnell, a League president from 1943 to 1944, added: "In state government changes come very slowly, particularly in a rich, conservative state like our own. I hope in the next thirty-five years this will be the [time period] in which we can have the most effect, both in supporting structural changes for better government, [and] in urging the appointment of intelligent and competent women in our governing bodies and in creating a climate in which such women can successfully run for office in our local and state government."

- Strong, too, was ahead of her time regarding women holding public office. It has taken longer than the year 1990 to achieve election parity for women. By 2019, hundreds of women had been elected to serve in local governments. Forty-four seats (29 percent) of the 2019 Iowa General Assembly were held by women, and Iowa that year had a female governor and female United States senator—both firsts!

- LWVIA President Mary Rae Bragg (2016–19) of Dubuque, a retired journalist, said in her last President's Message to Iowa Leaguers: "And don't let anyone tell you gender doesn't matter. It doesn't take a rocket scientist to figure out that issues inherently important to women are going to be given more attention when their voices are being heard in the assembly. Or, as my favorite T-shirt says, 'If you aren't at the table, you're on the menu!' … So make sure to remind the female governor, senator, and members of the General Assembly that they need to be conscious of being a voice for women who have been underrepresented for far too long."

- In the 1960s, the League advocated for judicial reform to increase nonpartisanship. In the 1970s, the League introduced the open meetings concept as part of its commitment to citizens' rights for transparency by government decision-makers.

- The League introduced to the public and Iowa legislators the terms "land use" and "water quality" in the 1980s as members worked for regulations to protect the environment. In the 1990s, the League introduced issues relating to mental health services in the state, as well as the need for campaign finance reform.

- The new century began with the League learning about elder abuse and lobbying for public knowledge and protection. The organization also introduced Iowa voters to an electronic means to easily access candidates' positions on various topics. The website, Vote411.org, is available to League members and the public alike (see Chapter 11).

Frank Miller cartoon. "Women in Politics! Women in Sports! Women in Everything! Next We'll Have Women in This Club!" Permission granted by the *Des Moines Register*

"… we are meeting some part of our obligations to the rest of the world when we work to make our democracy here in the United States an encouragement to democracy elsewhere. For all history teaches us that it is in the cradle of democracy that the will to peace is nurtured." —Margaret Wells, LWVUS president, contained in the "Historian's Report" by Mrs. T. John Jones for the 19th convention of the Iowa League of Women Voters in Sioux City, April 1939.

In support of Mrs. Wells' statement about the League's efforts to make democracy work, not just for our citizens, but as an example to the world, the following paragraphs present a more definitive look at the work of the League of Women Voters of Iowa across nine decades. Specific legislation the League impacted is contained in narrative form in Chapter 8 and in the Legislation Appendix. The League's persistence across time was required to achieve the goal of passing laws or modifying the Iowa Code. Other League activities summarized here are for the purpose of informing the public about relevant issues of the time.

The 1930s. The League supported vocational training or adjustment training for adults who were unemployed in order to make them employable. The organization also backed a renewed Juvenile Court system, as well as an improved probation system. Because the League believed that some county and state positions should not be elected but appointed based on qualifications, such as sheriffs and auditors, they successfully campaigned for a "short ballot," which was one of several aspects of a state referendum. In March 1931, the League designed and installed a bronze tablet in the Iowa Historical Building honoring twenty-four women who worked for suffrage and the advancement of women.

The 1940s. The League sponsored a Cost-of-Living Conference in March 1947, with over three hundred people from thirty-five communities across Iowa in attendance. The aim was to discuss government control of prices and rents through the Office of Price Administration (OPA) within the Office for Emergency Management. OPA was established in 1941, after the outbreak of World War II, and later moved to the Office of the Housing Expeditor. An "Iowa Voters' Handbook," dedicated to Carrie Chapman Catt, was created and distributed across the state. The state League encouraged local Leagues such as Davenport (later Scott County) to begin radio broadcasts about current issues, similar to what the National League had begun the decade before. Members also created *Broadsides*, one-page flyers about various issues the League was working on, to distribute to local Leagues and communities without a League. This concept subsequently was replicated by Leagues across the United States.

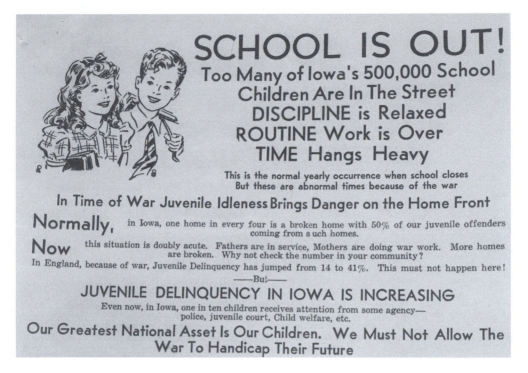

SCHOOL IS OUT!
Too Many of Iowa's 500,000 School Children Are In The Street
DISCIPLINE is Relaxed
ROUTINE Work is Over
TIME Hangs Heavy

This is the normal yearly occurrence when school closes
But these are abnormal times because of the war

In Time of War Juvenile Idleness Brings Danger on the Home Front

Normally, in Iowa, one home in every four is a broken home with 50% of our juvenile offenders coming from s uch homes.

Now this situation is doubly acute. Fathers are in service, Mothers are doing war work. More homes are broken. Why not check the number in your community?

In England, because of war, Juvenile Delinquency has jumped from 14 to 41%. This must not happen here!

——But——

JUVENILE DELINQUENCY IN IOWA IS INCREASING

Even now, in Iowa, one in ten children receives attention from some agency— police, juvenile court, Child welfare, etc.

Our Greatest National Asset Is Our Children. We Must Not Allow The War To Handicap Their Future

Iowa League of Women Voters *Broadside* flyer No. 4.

The 1950s. The League worked for the establishment of a Legislative Council to assist legislators and studied needed reforms to the judicial selection process. The organization also supported the council-manager form of local government and voiced concerns for racial equality, public education financing, fairness in government, and clean water. Members started studies of those last four issues that carried into the next decade.

The 1960s. The League organized a Conference for Joint Action on Community Problems in April 1969 in Waterloo. Then-League President Nan Waterman (1969–71) of Muscatine, who later served on the national League board, secured a Ford Foundation grant to fund the conference. Mrs. Waterman had attended two other such conferences and felt a gathering of community leaders would have a positive impact on the racial issues in Waterloo, as well as in other urban areas of Iowa. Mrs. Frank Williams, a National League director, led much of the conference, talking about and demonstrating active listening as a prerequisite for understanding. Mrs. Robert Thayer, an attendee, summarized two concepts reiterated throughout the discussions—concepts as relevant today as then:

> No one can determine for you how much of yourself you are
> going to commit to the struggle for equality and justice. But

upon having made a commitment, it is not a sometimes thing; it will not be easy, but because it is right, will provide its own reward.

None of us can be successful in eradicating prejudice in the white community until we have as individuals developed a security within ourselves concerning our own identity. Then we must search for the existing practices of racism, we must see it working to degrade, we must admit its eroding destruction, and accept our share of the blame in perpetuating it. Only then can we effectively and with conviction set about to help and support the victims of racism.

An often asked but never answered question at the conference was: Can a middle-class, white, procedure-oriented organization find true relevance in a rapidly changing and explosive society?

Iowa Leagues have been addressing that question in the fifty years since the 1969 conference as we have dealt with societal changes and their impact on volunteer organizations and communities. The issues of white privilege, prejudice, and racism are still very relevant and prevalent in U.S. society. These issues are reflected in books such as Debby Irving's *Waking Up White (and Finding Myself in the Story of Race)* (2014, Elephant Room Press), a book some Leagues have used for community reads and discussions.

The 1970s. The League monitored Title IX statewide and promoted greater public awareness of aspects of revenue sharing. The organization also studied statewide daycare needs, "made 'land use' a household word, and had a dramatic impact on the Iowa reapportionment process." (5)

The 1980s. The League completed community and state profiles documenting unmet needs for food, housing, income assistance, and health care. The organization also sponsored Iowa's first live statewide NBC-affiliated telecast of a gubernatorial debate October 11, 1982. League President Mona Martin (1981–83) of Davenport reported, "Since the League had never done such an event, the who, why, when, where, and how much [it would cost] all had to be discovered." In addition, the state League organized a five-state conference held in August 1984 in the Illinois/Iowa Quad-Cities—Agriculture's Stake in World Trade. Organizers secured grants from Deere & Company, Monsanto, Burlington Northern Foundation, Pioneer Hi-Bred International, Land O'Lakes, CIBA-GEIGY, Funk Seeds, National Oats Co., and Beatrice Agri-Products Division. Mary Garst of the Garst Company and Chet Randolph, host of IPTV's "Market to Market," were panel moderators for twelve speakers from Washington, D.C., including Secretary of Agriculture John Rusling Block. Other speakers came from Harvard, Purdue, the University of Illinois, and the University of Minnesota, as well as New Mexico and Dijon, France.

Frank Miller cartoon from July 11, 1978. "I don't trust women drivers!" Permission granted by the *Des Moines Register*.

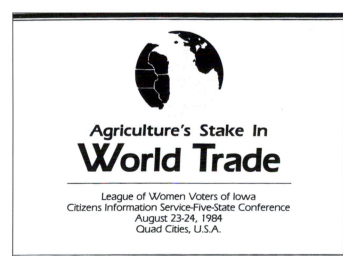

Five-state Agriculture's Stake in World Trade conference.

This productive decade included a number of activities funded by the League of Women Voters of Iowa Citizens Information Service. At the time, this arm of the League could receive tax-deductible contributions for educational projects (now the depository for such contributions is the League's Education Fund). One such project was a series of seminars on citizen participation in government, titled "Democracy is not a Spectator Sport," held at area community colleges via the now-outdated Iowa Communications Network. The League published "School Finance, the Iowa Foundation Program: A Guide Through the Iowa Code" and "Earmarking Taxes in Iowa." The organization did a survey of Iowa public schools' compliance with the one-person, one-vote principle, which resulted in a change to the reapportionment of school districts. The League also sponsored thirty-two "SAVE OUR SOIL" billboards throughout the state; distributed the "I-SAVE" pamphlet explaining Iowa's home energy audit program; and presented local programs for parents and educators clarifying the Juvenile Justice Code (which could now be done via internet connectivity unavailable in the 1980s).

The 1990s. Minnette Doderer, longtime League member and veteran legislator, described the League's impact on state government in 1993 at a Johnson County League meeting: "I don't think you're taking enough credit for what the League did at the state level. We were instrumental in judicial reform; we were way ahead of the curve in state district reapportionment—we spearheaded that! We were way ahead when we lobbied for the team provision [governor and lieutenant governor running as a team from the same political party] in the 1960s. We tried shortening the ballot. We got four-year terms for all state offices. We reformed state government just like we did local governments!" (6)

Well, the League did take credit during this decade, and rightfully so, for the League of Women Voters of Iowa and Cornell College's website gift to the Iowa Legislature. Two years of volunteer work by Professor Jim Freeman of Cornell College in Mount Vernon, the spouse of 1993–95 State League President Abbi Swanson, resulted in the design of a website for LWVIA and then the creation of the first state website for the Legislature. It was turned over to the Legislature on the seventy-sixth anniversary of the founding of the League of Women Voters of the United States. The Iowa Senate formally recognized the gift with Concurrent Resolution No. 114 (House Concurrent Resolution 118), thanking Dr. Freeman and the League for the significant contribution to the state, affording citizens a greater opportunity to access laws and legislation for their participation in our democratic system of government. Pending legislation, bills, and amendments can be tracked and identified by number, using keyword searches, or using House and Senate journals. The website is updated daily. Hyperlinks to the Iowa

Code and other state information are included, along with information about the representatives and senators in the Legislature. There is a virtual tour of the Iowa Capitol created by Dr. Freeman as well. *What a gift! What a service to the public! What a League! Check it out at www. legis.iowa.gov.*

Also in this decade of League action, members advocated for universal and affordable health care, including mental health care and funding; provided public education on household hazardous materials; continued work on campaign finance reform with a traveling display for libraries and communities; and continued advocacy for children at risk. The League also studied and developed a position on Iowa sentencing and corrections and began a longstanding collaboration with the American Civil Liberties Union (ACLU). The League and ACLU worked together to defeat the reinstatement of the death penalty in Iowa in 1998, as well as in subsequent years. Then-LWVIA Executive Director Marla Sheffler of the Metro Des Moines League, prior to the Des Moines LWVIA office closing, coordinated the effort against the death penalty. Ms. Sheffler went on to become LWVIA president from 2005 to 2007.

The 2000s. Iowa League Board members and other local Leaguers were invited to travel to Bosnia to help set up nonpartisan national elections and oversee them. Many went, including former LWVIA President Jan Beran (1995–97) of Ames and her husband. The League distributed statewide the pamphlet "More Sunlight: A Review of Electronic Filing and Disclosure"; studied domestic abuse and its ramifications for needed services and funding; and created a traveling display about campaign finance reform that went out to Iowa libraries, community gathering places, and local Leagues, in addition to sharing the information with neighboring states.

The 2010s. "The Board and I moved the League into the twenty-first century … by hiring an accountant, hiring a webpage manager, obtaining liability insurance for the state League and all local Leagues, and beginning the use of the online voter information site Vote411.org by local Leagues," said Bonnie Pitz, LWVIA president from 2012 to 2015. The League also established a collaboration with and membership in the Environmental Council; nominated Carrie Chapman Catt for a plaque on the Women of Achievement Bridge in downtown Des Moines with League members attending the dedication; received the 2017 Governor Harold E. Hughes Award in recognition of League advocacy to prevent the reinstatement of the death penalty in Iowa; and received the 2016 Edward S. Allen Award from the ACLU of Iowa for support of voting rights and for filing an amicus brief in the Griffin v. Pate ex-felon voting rights case. In the Griffin case, the League and others argued that it was unconstitutional to revoke the voting rights of Iowa resident Kelli Jo Griffin because of a past drug-related offense. The Iowa Supreme Court disagreed, ruling that the state's policy of permanent disenfranchisement for all citizens with felony convictions does not violate the state constitution (see Chapter 8 felon rights).

League members stand outside the Iowa Capitol in support of the amicus brief filed in Griffin v. Pate. The Brennan Center, on behalf of the League, wrote the brief on the ex-felon voting rights case before the Iowa Supreme Court.

In 2019, the LWVIA was involved in two projects funded by the national League: For the People Act and People Powered Fair Maps. The For the People Act grant supported a nationwide ad and postcard campaign demanding a hearing on the S.949 democracy reform bill, passed in the U.S. House in March 2019 and awaiting action in the U.S. Senate. The act's provisions address public campaign funding; bipartisan redistricting, which has occurred in Iowa since the 1970s; same-day voter registration; and automatic voter registration. These voting rights measures have wide support among the American public and a successful track record in many states.

The People Powered Fair Maps grant is a national redistricting program focused on the creation of fair political maps nationwide, in which the Iowa reapportionment process could be a model. For the last fifty years, Iowa congressional and legislative districts have been mapped in a non-partisan manner based on a constitutional amendment and statutory law. Therefore, the LWVUS grant dollars are being used for civic engagement and education on the much-lauded Iowa reapportionment process, as well as a campaign on the importance of an accurate census count. The census results provide the basis not only for representation in Congress and the Iowa General Assembly, but also for the calculation of millions in federal dollars that will come to Iowa for the next ten years.

The Values Leaguers Hold Dear

To accomplish the League work identified above and the legislation the League has worked to pass throughout the last century, either alone or in collaboration with other organizations, required monumental efforts (see Chapter 8). Certain values guide League members in these efforts. These values were well-stated in Mona Martin's presidential address at the 1983 League State Convention:

> First, we believe in the dual purpose of the League to educate ourselves and other citizens in the democratic process, and to take informed action to influence the formulation and outcomes of public policy.
>
> We believe that the strength of the League resides in its members who work as volunteers, primarily through the basic unit of League organization, the local League.
>
> We believe that leaders of the League, like our elected officials, should be responsive and accountable to our constituents, and should, in speaking for the League, reflect not only membership agreement and understanding, but the willingness of individual members to corroborate what the leaders say with action.
>
> We believe each level of the League should reinforce the others in symbiotic fashion, creating a whole that's greater than the sum of its local, state, and national parts.
>
> We believe that every member should have the opportunity to share in making decisions and the opportunity to learn, through training and experience in the democratic process.
>
> We believe that different points of view should be encouraged and allowed to compete.
>
> And, finally, we believe in doing things the right way, as well as doing the right things, because we take pride and satisfaction in the quality of our work as volunteers in public service.

Then and Now: Hats Off, Pants On

1915 Iowa Equal Suffrage Association Board, State Historical Society, Des Moines.

2017–19 League of Women Voters of Iowa Board of Directors.

Men in the League

In 1972, the League of Women Voters of the United States at its Biennial Convention voted to open membership to men. The next year, the first man to join the Iowa League was then-Governor Robert Ray, a Republican known as a centrist and lauded for working across the aisle. He frequently told people that the only way he could do the job of governor was to listen to everybody, consider the options, and know that there would be flak to deal with after his decisions. Mary Louise Smith (see Biographies Appendix) said of him: "People call him an odd mix of fiscal conservatism and sensitivity to social issues." (7)

During his five terms in office (1969–1983), he signed legislation and issued executive orders on issues that the League worked for or were related to League positions. As *Gazette* columnist Todd Dorman wrote at Governor Ray's death in 2018, "Robert Ray's record was built to last." (8) And most of it has.

Signed Legislation*(*indicates LWVIA position or support)

A new school aid formula* that reduced the burden on local property taxes; collective bargaining for public employees; the renowned non-partisan redrawing of congressional and legislative boundaries*; the removal of sales tax on food and prescription drugs; broader government transparency for open meetings and open records*; reorganization of state government, including the creation of the Department of Transportation and the Iowa Department of Natural Resources; reorganization of the state's judicial system*, bringing all courts under state control, ending the system of municipal- and county-run courts, and scrapping the justice-of-the-peace network*; the creation of the Iowa Commission on the Status of Women*; and his favorite piece of legislation, the "bottle bill"* that began recycling in the state and greatly impacted the environment*.

Executive Orders (* indicates LWVIA position or support)

No. 17, energy conservation in state buildings and vehicles, 1973*; No. 21, Iowa Council on Children, 1976 and 1978*; No. 23, Governor's Science Advisory Council, 1977; No. 27, Iowa Task Force on Government Ethics, 1977*; No. 39, Iowa Council for Children, Youth, and Families, 1980 and 1982*; No. 46, further initiatives such as affirmative action and equal employment opportunities in state governmental programs, 1982*; and No. 48, orderly use and development of land and related natural resources, 1983*.

Governor Ray, though not a radical, did take risks in his support for the Equal Rights Amendment* (January 2020 ratification by the 38th state, though after 1982 extended deadline—presently in the hands of Congress); legalized abortion*; the three-day waiting period for the purchase of a handgun; job training for inmates to prepare them for life after incarceration*; and his opposition to the death penalty*.

Governor Ray also is remembered for the passage of the Iowa Burials Protection Act of 1976, the first legislative act in the United States that specifically protected American Indian remains. He also is responsible for the relocation of thousands of Asian refugees following the Vietnam War by gaining special permission from U.S. Citizenship and Immigration Services for their relocation to Iowa.

Governor Robert Ray in 1974, State Historical Society, Des Moines.

The other men who joined the League along with Governor Ray, as reported in the *Des Moines Register* on February 18, 1973, were:

Des Moines—Ray Murphy (husband of a Leaguer), James Vickery, and Don Willis, insurance company executives; attorneys Lynn K. Vrobrich and Robert Mannheimer (husband of a Leaguer); J.A. MacCallister, telephone company executive; and college professor Desmond Bragg.

Iowa City—University of Iowa President Willard Boyd; University of Iowa professors Donald Bryant and Richard Lloyd-Jones; and William Hubbard, a former mayor of Iowa City (all married to Leaguers, with Professor Lloyd-Jones married to 1971–74 LWVIA President Jean Lloyd-Jones—later a state legislator).

Grinnell—Paul Kiesel, retired sales and engineering executive, and Grinnell College professors Charles Cleaver and Joseph Wall (all married to Leaguers).

Sioux City—Paul Berger, mayor of Sioux City.

Black Hawk-Bremer—local League reported that Jon Crews, mayor of Cedar Falls at the time, was the first man to join the then-Waterloo-Cedar Falls League in the 1970s. He was followed by Bill Teaford, husband of LWVIA President Jane Teaford (1979–81)—later a state legislator.

But, in the years before male members of Leagues, many men (and families) got involved in the League activities of their spouses (or mothers). In the early 1960s, the George W.S. Smith family of Oskaloosa got involved in the creation of "A Woman's Place," a 32-frame filmstrip with recorded narration explaining what the League is, how it came to be, and why. Mr. Smith, president of Ideal Manufacturing, provided technical help for his wife's project. Their children, Ellen and Jim, got involved with research and captions for the artwork that was rendered by an Ottumwa artist. The project was first viewed in 1963 at the state League's convention in Cedar Rapids, where the national League president saw it. Attendees' positive response to "A Woman's Place" resulted in the national League's adoption of production to make it available to all local Leagues in the nation. Here are some of the filmstrip slides:

When a woman joins the league, her dues make her a member of the local, state and national league. She meets in discussion groups, choosing issues the members decide to study, then act upon.

Slides from "A Woman's Place" filmstrip created in the late 1960s by an Oskaloosa League member and her family.

League action includes testifying at public hearings, use of public forums, panel discussions, mass media, league publications and letters to public officials.

. . . Association in its last 20 years. Women had worked for the vote not just to HAVE it but to achieve goals. As the Suffrage Association grew into the League of Women Voters, they went to work . . .

Other examples of male League members or families in the League include Don Maxam of Pella, whose wife Elsie was honored in 1994 with the Carrie Chapman Catt Earth Award for her work with the Earth Day Committee and her continual efforts to recycle, reuse, and restore. In that same League, membership was a family affair for Don and Helen Boertje and their daughter, and for Gretchen and Hutch Bearce and their daughter, Kate Bearce. And in Muscatine, police officer Rob Yant joined his wife, Karen, as a League member, later becoming the first male president of that League in 1994.

Some League members have made exceptional contributions to the state of Iowa, which is the goal of the work of the League: inform and advocate for critical issues and work for change that will improve the lives of our citizens. Dr. Jim Freeman, Cornell mathematics professor and a member at the time of the League in Mount Vernon (now a unit of the Linn County League), created the first website for the Iowa Legislature (shared above, "1990s").

Today there are male League members in all eleven Iowa local Leagues, and men make up nearly 20 percent of the total state League membership.

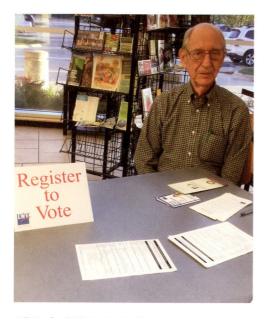

Bill Teaford, Black Hawk-Bremer League and spouse of former Legislator Jane Teaford, registering voters in 2017 at the Cedar Falls Public Library.

Gary Kaufman, Metro Des Moines League, managing a 2015 fundraising auction.

Chapter 7

Taking Action ...

Advocacy and Lobbying

AUTHOR JON MEACHAM reminds us of the obligations of citizenship in a republic: paying attention, gathering factual information, expressing opinions, and casting ballots. These responsibilities call to mind Theodore Roosevelt's directive: "The first duty of an American citizen is that he shall work in politics; his second duty is that he shall do that work in a practical manner; and his third is that it shall be done in accord with the highest principles of honor and justice." (1) President Roosevelt was talking about citizens engaging in government, being knowledgeable about issues, and letting decision-makers know where they stand. This is advocacy.

In addition to educating citizens, the League engages in advocacy and lobbying to achieve its goals of generating support for positions aimed at creating or changing government policies and practices. That activism stems from positions developed after a thorough study of issues. Armed with credible data and information from such a study, and through contact with decision-makers at the relevant level of government (a city council, county board, regional authority, Iowa Legislature, or Congress), informed citizens can effect change (see Chapters 8 and 9).

> "The League of Women Voters taught me that you [must] have outside pressure on the Legislature; they're not going to do it unless they hear people out there, voters, saying 'We need this.'"—former legislator Jean Lloyd-Jones (Iowa House 1979–87, Iowa Senate 1987–95), who also served as president of the League of Women Voters of Iowa (1971–74), Iowa City

Advocacy

The Alliance for Justice defines advocacy as "any action that speaks in favor of, recommends, argues for a cause, supports or defends, or pleas on behalf of others." (2) (The Alliance for Justice is "a progressive judicial advocacy group" that was formed in 1979 "to monitor federal judicial appointments [and] work to ensure that the federal judiciary advances core constitutional values, preserves human rights and unfettered access to the courts, and adheres to the even-handed administration of justice for all Americans." [www.afj.org])

Iowa State Capitol: Under the Golden Dome

Many examples of advocacy provided by the alliance are consistent with long-standing League advocacy activities:

- Assembling a large group concerned about the issue your organization is working on;
- Providing information and data that your study has generated and creating educational tools for the public and decision-makers, such as brochures, flyers, and articles for newspapers or websites;
- Organizing a rally, a parade, or another public event with speakers on the issue and literature to distribute; and
- When registering voters or encouraging voters to go to the polls, informing them about the issues and where to find information about candidates, their positions, and incumbent voting records.

League members commonly engage in the following advocacy activities as well:

- Creating petitions and obtaining signatures to submit to decision-makers;

- Writing letters and emails to legislators about issues or legislation that is under consideration, often in response to an Action Alert sent out from LWVIA or LWVUS emphasizing an immediate need to contact lawmakers; and
- Appearing at sessions of decision-makers, such as city council and county board meetings, as well as visiting the Iowa Legislature or traveling to Washington, D.C., for congressional sessions. Public meetings typically allow time for citizens' input, and individuals can make appointments to speak directly to state legislators and members of Congress. They also can attend committee and subcommittee meetings that are open to the public.

Also, many Leagues periodically host Legislative Forums for their state legislators to share information with constituents and answer questions. These meetings also can be initiated by legislators or members of Congress to provide feedback on their work and take questions from attendees.

Advocacy Versus Lobbying

In addition to grassroots advocacy activities, organizations can employ one or more paid or volunteer lobbyists to interact with state legislators or members of Congress. "Not all advocacy is lobbying, but all lobbying is advocacy." (3)

Former LWVIA President (1979–81) Jane Teaford of Cedar Falls, a member of the Iowa House from 1985 to 1993, commented on League lobbyists: "… [such] a lobbyist can be counted on to provide accurate and current information, based on comprehensive study and non-partisanship … [and in general] lobbying is an honorable occupation."

Lobbying is the act of attempting to influence, through written or oral communication, government decision-makers to create legislation or conduct an activity that will meet the goals of an organization. A lobbyist is a designated representative of an organization whose purpose or goal is to encourage the passage, defeat, approval, veto, or legislative modification of a rule or an executive order before the General Assembly or a state agency.

"If you know what you're talking about, people will listen. Most legislators don't have a lot of background on all the issues that come before them [so they need to have the facts]."—Joan Lipsky, Iowa House 1967–79, Cedar Rapids

Understanding Decision-makers in Government

A lot of what legislators do to better serve constituents is to learn about issues outside their sphere of experience or training. An effective lobbyist often acts as a teacher, knowing that adults commit to learning when they see the relevance. As learners, adults need more repetition than they like to admit. Therefore, materials used to educate about an issue need to be revisited after the initial presentation with a handout, fact sheet, or website, all featuring easy-to-read information, charts, graphics, and even humor.

Also, anyone working with decision-makers benefits from an understanding of the six types of power. Of the six, lobbyists and their clients have only three:

- Referent, where person B (the legislator) sees person A (the lobbyist or advocate) as similar to herself or holding like values;
- Expert, where person B (the legislator) perceives person A (the lobbyist or advocate) as having knowledge or expertise B does not; and
- Informational, where information (from the League) has the power, not the person who gives it out.

The League of Women Voters and its informed members have a long history of expert and informational power with decision-makers at all levels of government. And often an organization, its members, or a lobbyist can establish referent power with decision-makers on certain issues if similarity of values can be established.

One type of power legislators and other decision-makers have by virtue of their elected positions is legitimate power—the legal or authoritative ability to make or control decisions. The other two types of power have no place in the relationships between those attempting to influence decision-makers and those individuals tasked with decision-making: reward (person A bestowing benefits or awards on person B) and coercive (person A dispensing or withholding benefits from person B), both reflected in restrictions on lobbyists and the professional ethics of elected officials.

Two Types of Lobbying

The Internal Revenue Service (IRS Reg. §56.4911-2) defines two distinct types of lobbying activities: direct lobbying communication and grassroots lobbying communication. Direct lobbying refers to oral or written communication with a legislator, her staff, or another government employee who may participate in the formulation of legislation that contains a view or position favorable to the organization the lobbyist is representing. Grassroots lobbying is an attempt to influence legislation by influencing the public's opinions. Oral or written communication about specific legislation or an issue is presented to encourage the lawmaker to act, including contacting other legislators or decision-makers.

History of LWVIA Lobbyists

Initially, volunteer lobbyists represented the League of Women Voters of Iowa at the state Capitol. Fourteen have been identified: Johnie Hammond who later served in both the House and Senate of the Iowa Legislature from 1983 to 2003, Betty Kitzman, and Barbara Koerber, Ames; Mary Garst, Coon Rapids (inducted into the Iowa Women's Hall of Fame in 1981); Marjorie Engeldinger, Sherry Hutchison, Louise Moon (LWVIA president 1975–79), Dannie Rosenfeld, Marilyn Staples, and Lois Tucker, all of Des Moines; Jane Wallerstedt, Indianola; Susan "Suki" Cell, Mount Vernon; Joan Lucas, Pella; and Diane Brandt, Waterloo, who later served in the Iowa House from 1975 to 1983.

Lobbyists sometimes enjoyed less-than-welcoming receptions in the early years of League lobbying in Des Moines. Mrs. Moon recalled a comment from an Iowa House legislator addressed to her, Mrs. Engeldinger, and Mrs. Tucker one morning in the 1960s while they were observing a committee meeting: "Why don't you three go home and wash the breakfast dishes and make the beds?" They deflected this attempt at intimidation and disparagement by replying they had already done all those tasks before leaving their homes! Lieutenant Governor Arthur Neu made a more flattering statement about Mrs. Moon in 1977: "Louise leans so far over the balcony when she is interested in a piece of legislation that someday I'm afraid she may tumble over!"

Lobbyist Judie
Hoffman

Since 1986, the League of Women Voters of Iowa has retained a paid lobbyist to conduct both direct and grassroots lobbying. The first was longtime League member Judie Hoffman of Ames, who served the League for twenty-four years (1986–2009). Senator Herman Quirmbach, Ames, commented about his friend, who was an Ames City Council colleague from 1998 to 2003: "A public servant in the best definition of the term … anybody who held her up as the ideal to emulate would be making an excellent choice." (4) Kari Carney, executive director of 1000 Friends of Iowa, a statewide nonprofit organization focused on land use education, said she was glad to have had the opportunity to work with Ms. Hoffman on farming, environmental, and economic justice issues over the years.

After her retirement as the LWVIA lobbyist, Ms. Hoffman remained an active member of the Ames & Story County League and a member of the LWVIA Criminal and Juvenile Justice Committee. Before her death in 2017, she was awarded the Ames & Story County League's inaugural Making Democracy Work Award, as well as the Iowans Against the Death Penalty Harold Hughes Award. As one of her sons said at her passing, "The moral arc of the universe bends closer to justice, thanks to our mom!" His comment was a paraphrase of the following:

"The arc of the moral universe is long, but it bends toward justice." This metaphor is attributed to Theodore Parker (1810–1860), a Unitarian minister, abolitionist, and reformer. He was identified as a transcendentalist, and several quotations from his sermons were used by Abraham Lincoln and Martin Luther King Jr. in their writings and speeches. Interestingly, early suffragists Julia Ward Howe and Elizabeth Cady Stanton were in his Boston congregation in 1846!

Tasks of the Lobbyist in Direct Lobbying

Before each legislative session, the LWVIA Board, in consultation with the lobbyist, prioritizes issues that are expected to come before the Legislature. When the session begins, the lobbyist talks to legislators, staff, other lobbyists, and legislative liaisons and provides written materials on the issues in bills introduced. The lobbyist also provides testimony to House and Senate subcommittees and committees in support of or in opposition to a bill. The following is the first two paragraphs of a two-page, single-spaced, typewritten script of one of Judie Hoffman's many testimonies during her time as a League lobbyist.

September 21, 1989, Interim Committee on
Comprehensive Campaign Reform

I am Judie Hoffman of the League of Women Voters of Iowa. I appreciate the opportunity to testify before [this committee]. Campaign finance reform is an issue the League has worked on for over 15 years because of its continuing concern for open and honest elections and maximum citizen participation in the political process.

There are three major issues involved in campaign finance reform. The first is control of spending and the attendant matter of public financing of campaigns. The second is limits on individual contributions and PACs, and the third is public disclosure of contributions and expenditures. All of these were addressed in a landmark U.S. Supreme Court case in 1976 in which the League participated.

League members who are well-versed on a topic can, of course, talk with legislators about an issue. They also can give testimony at General Assembly subcommittee or committee hearings when the LWVIA leadership and the lobbyist asks them to, provided they can get to Des Moines in time.

Other direct lobbying work includes attending legislative committees, subcommittees, and coalition meetings that are related to League positions; arranging meetings with legislative leaders, the governor, and staff as needed; and monitoring other issues of interest to LWVIA, which may be related to one or more League positions not previously identified as a top priority for lobbying.

Des Moines League member Karen Person gives testimony for the restoration of voting rights to felons upon completion of their sentences, a long-standing position of the League.

Tasks of Lobbyists in Grassroots Lobbying

Grassroots lobbying, or influencing non-legislators, involves a wider variety of activities than direct lobbying of decision-makers in government and takes up the majority of a lobbyist's time. Current LWVIA Lobbyist Amy Campbell's 2017–19 "LWVIA Scope of Work" documents her grassroots lobbying tasks.

1. Before the legislative session begins, the lobbyist emails the LWVIA Board and all local League presidents "Top Priorities for the Year," which have been determined by the board and the lobbyist. During the session, the lobbyist emails *Legislative Updates*. The newsletter presents information about bills that have been introduced and are in committee review, along with any action that has occurred. The lobbyist shares information about anticipated future action or bills and suggestions for League member advocacy action such as:

> "… ask the Senate Natural Resources and Environmental Committee for similar legislation to HF 181 [the expansion of Iowa's bottle redemption law] for consideration in the Senate."
> —*Legislative Updates* from February 10, 2019

The *Legislative Updates* provide all the information needed to contact a legislator—telephone number, email, and physical address—along with suggested talking points. Also included is a reminder of "Your Bill Tracker," compliments of Ms. Campbell's "Advocacy Cooperative," an easy-to-navigate resource at www.ialobby.com/billtracker/lwvia/ that tracks bills during the session. In addition, the *Updates* often include photos of meetings "under the Golden Dome," with pictures of legislators at work and people advocating for their positions and causes.

2. The lobbyist routinely informs League members across the state about an urgent need to communicate with their legislators through an Action Alert. This information originally was sent via phone calls but now is distributed by email. Here is an example of an Action Alert sent by Judie Hoffman in May 2003:

> "The Iowa Legislature is looking at making changes in the Iowa tax system that are not progressive and which the public has not had an opportunity to examine carefully. The League of Women Voters supports an equitable and flexible system of taxation. A tax should be evaluated primarily on equity, taxpayer ability to pay, and adequate yield. The League advocates a progressive income tax." Ms. Hoffman then listed five bullets as "talking points" to support the position. "... Contact your legislators and the Governor immediately and tell them you want a progressive income tax that is revenue-neutral. To obtain email addresses of the legislators, please visit the Iowa General Assembly website: www.legis.state.ia.us."

An Action Alert also can be a call to action for League members to come, if possible, to the Capitol for a committee hearing or floor debate in order to have a presence before legislators in support or opposition to a bill.

3. Among the lobbyist's other duties are developing legislative materials if League information materials are insufficient for a session or issue, and helping the LWVIA Board plan topics and speakers for two major events: the Issues Briefing meeting for all local League members and Capitol Lobby Day in Des Moines. The lobbyist also prepares the final session report to the LWVIA Board and local League presidents, as well as the annual LWVIA Convention/Council Report.

Read more on restrictions for lobbyists and what makes a good lobbyist in the Lobbying Appendix.

Chapter 8

Getting 'er Done ...

The Legislation the League has Worked to Pass

THIS CHAPTER CONTAINS the legislation and constitutional amendments the League of Women Voters of Iowa, either alone or in collaboration with other organizations, has worked to pass in the Iowa Legislature from 1922 to 2019. Included also are bills the League worked to defeat. The legislation is organized chronologically in six categories: Children and Families, Education, the Environment, Good Government, Human Rights, and Voting Rights.

This League work has had a significant impact on the lives of Iowans. League members Johnie Hammond (Ames & Story County) and Pat Harper (Black Hawk-Bremer), who both served in the Iowa Legislature (1983–2003 and 1985–2003, respectively), wrote the following introduction to this section in a tribute to Minnette Doderer. She was the longest-serving legislator in Iowa history as of this publication—thirty-two years—with a meeting room at the Iowa Capitol named for her.

> "Where but in Johnson County would you find a soul held in such high esteem that the county Democrats would hold a barbecue, a fundraiser, a roast, and a memorial all at the same time to honor their departed friend? Minnette Doderer was a talented, funny, brilliant, passionate, mischievous, compassionate, sensitive, one-of-a-kind person. She was dedicated to good, clean government, as evidenced by her long legislative record.
>
> "Minnette knew legislation and the Iowa Legislature better than most of her colleagues. She was a strong advocate for civil liberties and women's rights. She knew the hard work and negotiations needed to make progress toward equal rights for

women. She worked tirelessly for the Equal Rights Amendment, changing the language in the amendment the second time around from 'sex' to 'gender' to appease the conservatives. She was dedicated to gender equity in insurance premiums. She devoted a lot of energy to get the same rights and opportunities for women in prison as the male prisoners had. This involved working for equity in job training, educational opportunity, and health care. She was vigilant about women's reproductive rights, defending against attacks on abortion rights with vigorous speeches and introduction of amendments to negative legislation in the Iowa House. She was a champion for child welfare. Getting gender balance on state boards and commissions was another fight she took on. With all these issues, she worked with all parties that had the power to get things done. On issue after issue, Minnette's agenda was also the League's agenda."

Minnette Doderer

Identifying every piece of legislation the League has impacted over nearly a hundred years is like putting together a thousand-piece puzzle with several hundred pieces missing! Every effort has been made to find all such laws. However, records in a volunteer organization such as the League are not always complete, and archived laws at the Legislative Services Agency are not listed by topic or alphabetically and do not include the parties that lobbied for or supported the bill. Early bills passed by the Legislature did not always have House or Senate file numbers attached to them, and even in more recent years some bill topics are not easily decipherable as to topic. Also, on occasion, amendments unrelated to the core of a bill are added, and thus harder to identify. But even if all legislation was not found, there is plenty to read about the work of the League to improve the lives of Iowans (see Legislation Appendix for a listing of laws without a narrative).

I. Children and Families: It Takes a Village

Flora Dunlap, the first president of the League of Women Voters of Iowa, would be quite proud of the work Leaguers have done for children and families across the years. A protégé of Jane Addams, Dunlap was a social worker who reconstructed the Roadside Settlement House in Des Moines and was its head resident for eighteen years (see Chapter 2 Appendix). She may well have led the League's work in 1924 for passage of a bill establishing an Iowa Child Welfare Commission.

The following is legislation impacting the most vulnerable in our state—children, the poor, the mentally ill, and senior citizens.

Adoption of Children

Initial legislation pertaining to the adoption of children was passed in 1919, the same year the Nineteenth Amendment was ratified in Iowa. It was codified in Chapter 9 Section 6685-6689, before the League began work on this issue. League records indicate that in 1923, the organization had a concern for improving adoption laws, which may be reflected in the update of the Iowa Code in 1924 and again in 1927. Provision for a Welfare Commission was also passed in 1924. Further changes in Iowa adoption laws were reflected in the 1946 Iowa Code Chapter 600.1-9 and in the 1950 Iowa Code Chapter 600.1–10, refinements the League definitely pushed. The latter change added sealed adoption records to the Code, an increase from six to twelve months of residence in the adopted home before formal adoption, and private adoption hearings—all measures to protect the rights of the child.

The 1970s saw three pieces of legislation regarding adoption passed into Iowa law: 1) participation of the father, not just the mother, in the relinquishment process, which included counseling, before the termination of the rights of both parents; 2) simplification of the process for adopted children to gain access to legal records when of age, thus making it easier to find biological parents; and 3) a full, mandatory investigation of the adopting parents before a child could be placed in their home.

Child Abuse

The 1966 Iowa Code Chapter 235A.1–7 defined child abuse and contained much of the language offered by the League. HF 1251, passed in 1970, stated that children under the age of twelve could not be employed as migrant laborers in agriculture. This act built upon the Iowa Legislature's ratification in 1932 of the 1924 federal child labor constitutional amendment that was never sufficiently ratified. The amendment became unnecessary after passage of the 1938 federal Fair Labor Standards Act that regulated child labor.

1971 saw the expansion of Iowa Code Chapter 92.1–23 to include other restrictions on child labor. No person under fourteen could be employed or permitted to work with or without compensation in any occupation, except in the street trade occupations or migratory labor occupations; and twelve- to sixteen-year-olds could not work during regular school hours.

And in the 1980s, Senator Joy Corning helped pass bills outlawing physical abuse in schools and extending the statute of limitations on sexual abuse.

Childcare

The League supports programs, services, and policies at all levels of government to expand the supply of affordable, quality childcare for all who need it, in order to increase access to employment and education, and to prevent and reduce poverty. Proposed legislation in 1974 would have required licensing of all daycare centers, not just those receiving federal or state funds. Licensing requires subsequent state inspection, which is costly, so the League presented a compromise position to license facilities serving seven or more children. Those facilities serving fewer than seven children simply would be registered. The compromise passed (originally SF 569).

1999–2001 witnessed the passage of legislation requiring inspections of in-home childcare providers and updating regulations regarding the ratio of providers to children and the minimum size of facilities per child. And in 2002, the number of children allowed for a registered provider had to include the provider's own children who were home during the day.

The League has continually monitored the quality of childcare, based on valid data. An example is a 1997 bill that set the number of infants at four, in addition to four older children, who could be cared for by one person. Current ratios of adult caregivers to children are more restrictive at various age ranges: for infants six weeks to eighteen months, the ratio is 1:4; at twenty-seven months it is 1:6; at three years it is 1:8; at four years it is 1:12; and for five to nine years and age ten and over it is 1:15. More details can be found at daycare.com/iowa, including total number of children in care per facility or provider.

Further, the League worked for adequate funding of childcare centers to support low- and middle-income families, to improve facilities, to purchase new equipment, and to train staff (originally SF 434). This advocacy for childcare funding has been consistent across the years, such as in 1996, when the League was successful in garnering a 40 percent increase in funding, to $12.5 million. And in 1997, the League supported the increased reimbursement rates for registered and licensed providers, while maintaining rates for unregistered providers as an encouragement for them to become registered.

The League also has worked diligently to increase the amount of income above the federal poverty level that low-income families can earn and still qualify for childcare assistance, as seen in 1997, when the cutoff was raised to 125 percent of the federal poverty level and in 2000 to 140 percent. And by 2014, families earning up to 145 percent of the federal poverty level could meet a twenty-eight-hour minimum work threshold by working, going to school, or being in an approved training program (or a combination that reaches twenty-eight hours).

This Iowa legislation was an outgrowth of the 1990 federal Act for

Better Child Care, or ABC bill. It stipulated that adults participating in education, job training, or community work activities under the act were entitled to subsidized childcare. The federal act also allowed for an additional year of childcare during a parent's transition from welfare to work.

The health of children cared for in centers also has been a concern of Leaguers. Legislation in 2002 prohibited smoking in areas used by children during operating hours at a childcare home or facility, as established by a new category of childcare in Iowa—"Child Development Homes." And in 2003, legislation instituted mandatory background checks for sexual abuse charges for all childcare workers—a League concern for children's safety.

Domestic Violence

The LWVIA's 2001 position on domestic violence (www.lwvia.org) found the need for several changes to the legal and social support now given to victims of domestic violence, calling for "… a review of existing penalties for [the] perpetrator and working for more consistent enforcement of present laws." The League also supports increased funding for services in counseling, shelter, and education of victims and their families and encourages businesses to develop programs to educate and support their employees who are involved in domestic violence. Finally, the League urges the Department of Public Safety to publish statewide statistics related to domestic violence, a task currently cited only as an option in the Code of Iowa.

In 1997, the League helped secure passage of legislation that required a warning against domestic abuse to be placed on all Iowa marriage license certificates and applications. In 2000, after three years of work, League-member legislators Mona Martin and Maggie Tinsman shepherded through HF 2362, which established a Domestic Abuse Death Review Team. The team was charged with identifying causes and manners of deaths resulting from domestic abuse. The Iowa Legislature doubled funding for domestic violence and sexual assault victim services in 2013.

Early Intervention for Children at Risk

The League believes that early intervention and prevention measures are effective in helping children reach their potential, so it supports policies and programs at all levels of government that promote the well-being, encourage the full development, and ensure the safety of children. This includes child abuse and neglect prevention; teen pregnancy prevention; quality health care that includes nutrition and prenatal care; early childhood education; developmental services, emphasizing ages zero to three; family support services; and violence prevention.

In 1975, the Legislature funded through January 1976 the Governor's Task Force on Early Childhood Development. Legislation established a school-ready grant program for the ages zero to five population in 1998, giving local Iowa Empowerment Boards the flexibility to apply for funds for quality childcare programs, child development programs, and childcare assistance programs.

In 2004, the League supported the Healthy Families HOPES (Healthy Opportunities for Parents to Experience Success) grant program, an intensive in-home program for young parents of children from birth to five (or until goals are met). The HOPES program builds parenting skills and confidence, connects families to community resources, assists with budgeting and finding quality childcare, and provides guidance for continuing education.

Family Planning Services

Legislation was passed in 1965, and then written into Iowa Code 234.21-28 in 1966, that provided family planning services only to a targeted population. The law stipulated that services could be offered to parents or to married people who were public assistance recipients, where it was deemed necessary by the state Department of Social Welfare to provide, pay for, and offer family planning and birth control services.

The League has monitored such services and lobbied for increased funding for fifty years. The organization last achieved success in 2008, when $750,000 was included in the budget—funding that would help 170,000 low-income women access contraceptive services and reduce unintended pregnancies. Even with that level of funding, Iowa ranked near the bottom of all states in availability of contraceptive services.

According to a current Guttmacher Institute report (www.guttmacher.org), states have become more successful in enacting public funding restrictions for family planning. Some states, including Iowa, have made providers' eligibility for state funding contingent on meeting certain conditions, such as not offering abortion services, even if such services are provided without using state funds. Increasingly, states are seeking to deny funds even to entities that do not provide abortions but offer counseling or referral for abortion. And a number of states now allocate funds through a priority system that either disadvantages or wholly excludes safety-net health centers affiliated with clinics that provide abortion. These restrictions typically apply to state family planning funds or federal family planning funds that pass through the state treasury.

Some states, again including Iowa, have gone so far as to end their joint state-federal Medicaid family planning expansion programs in favor of entirely state-funded "spin-off" programs. These state-funded programs cover many of the same services as the Medicaid family planning expansions, but they exclude providers that offer abortion services. Other states now are seeking to prevent safety-net health centers from receiving other types of public funds intended to address a wide range of public health concerns, such as infant mortality, sexually-transmitted infections, breast and cervical cancer, and domestic and sexual violence. This policy discriminates against low-income individuals who lack private insurance for such services.

Health

The League, under its platform of meeting basic human needs, believes access to health care includes preventive and primary care, maternal and child health care, emergency and catastrophic care, nursing home care, health and sex education programs, and nutrition programs. Advocating for Iowans' health constituted some of the League's earliest efforts. As an example, in 1923, SF 513 prohibited the sale of any milk, cream, skim milk, buttermilk, condensed or evaporated milk, powdered or desiccated milk, condensed skim milk, or any of the fluid derivatives of any of these products to which had been added any fat or oil other than milk fat, such as coconut oil. How times have changed!

1923 also saw the passage of Iowa legislation enabling the state to accept funds under the Sheppard-Towner Act, a federal matching funds program in effect from 1921 to 1927. The act provided up to one-half the state's cost of instructional guides for maternity hygiene and infant care through public health nurses, visiting nurses, consultation centers, and childcare conferences. Educational materials on prenatal care could be created and distributed with the funds, and regulation and licensure of midwives was promoted. The federal legislation and the states' implementation of it is lauded for spurring dramatic decreases in infant mortality.

"Gin marriage" regulation was a hot topic in the late 1920s. Dorothy Schramm, a founder of the Burlington League, may have written the following: "After WWI, with the relaxation of tension for the conflict, there was an accompanying relaxation of the code of morals of young people ... with plenty of money, and [bootleg] liquor and marriage licenses easy to obtain, many hasty or 'gin marriages' occurred. Social welfare workers became alarmed at the possible results." They worried the trend would lead to divorce, unwanted children, even domestic abuse. It was thought that a waiting period between the application for a marriage license and the date of the marriage would make a hasty marriage more difficult.

Neighboring states Illinois, Minnesota, Nebraska, and Wisconsin already had waiting period laws, and they wanted Iowa to have one as well to keep their young people from crossing the state line to get married quickly or under the influence of alcohol. The state League's Legislative Committee began work in 1930 on a waiting period bill. It was crafted, reviewed by an attorney paid for by the League, and presented to legislators for their consideration. The bill, with a five-day waiting period, was passed in 1932, but it was repealed the next year due to opposition from florists and preachers.

In 1935, a bill directed toward the same end was drafted, but with a three-day waiting period and a required health examination. It passed and was in effect for several decades. Only the three-day waiting period survived to present times. No health examination or blood test, the latter a requirement from a 1941 pre-marital health bill, is required now.

1939 witnessed the creation of Iowa Code Chapter 109, Venereal Diseases, which included requirements for general reporting, blood tests for pregnant women, and reporting on birth certificates for syphilis, gonorrhea, and chancroid, a bacterial infection now rare in the United States. Isabel Elliott's bill also mandated that if the pregnant woman's test was positive, the child's father had to be tested as well.

In 1975, the Legislature established services for the deaf within the Department of Health (SF 223/HF 332). And legislation passed in 1977 required immunization of children for German measles, mumps, diphtheria, whooping cough, tetanus, and polio before entering school, with exceptions granted only for religious reasons.

1996 saw the passage of the so-called "drive-by delivery bill," which required insurers to allow a forty-eight-hour maternity stay for a regular delivery and a ninety-six-hour maternity stay for a C-section. Additional legislation that year tripled fines for minors purchasing alcohol and fines for owners of the liquor license and the clerk who made the sale.

In 1998, the Legislature passed Hawk-i Children's Health Care, covering children up to age nineteen from families with incomes too high to qualify for Medicaid, up to 133 percent of the federal poverty level. This program was partially funded by the federal Children's Health Insurance Program (CHIP) and covered routine checkups, immunizations, doctor visits, prescriptions, dental and vision care, lab and X-ray services, and inpatient and outpatient hospital care.

That same year, HF 2110 required single-pack cigarettes to be placed behind store counters so that children and young adults could not have easy access. It also prohibited advertising of cigarettes near playgrounds and schools. HF 204, passed in 1999, prohibited giving away cigarettes and tobacco products as free samples and banned promotional giveaways in concert with the sale of cigarettes and tobacco products, a tool often used to entice young people into using tobacco. And 2000 saw legislative action for the use of federal tobacco tax monies for health care.

In 2002, the League joined a coalition to preserve the $55 million federal tobacco settlement for Iowa. The money was used to raise the Hawk-i threshold to 200 percent of the federal poverty level and to add coverage for other health care needs, such as emergency medical services, epidemiology, substance abuse treatment, and expanded home health care services. And in 2007, the League worked for an increase in cigarette taxes from $0.36 per pack to $1.36, which took Iowa from one of the lowest tobacco tax states (seventeenth) to a little above average. Again, this tax money was used to pay for health care.

2012 witnessed the success of several health bills, including the passage of Iowa's Healthiest Child Initiative Implementation Plan, with the goal that Iowa children become the healthiest in the nation by 2020; and legislation to "modernize" HIV criminal transmission, which repealed one of the nation's toughest laws punishing perceived exposure to HIV and switched to one that is scientifically based. This law replaced a mandatory twenty-five-year prison sentence and lifetime sex offender status with a three-tiered system that decriminalizes most types of exposure, unless the intent to transmit is verified.

In 2013, Iowa expanded Medicaid after the passage of the federal Affordable Care Act. The Legislature created the Iowa Health and Wellness Plan as a hybrid Medicaid expansion, which included parity for mental health coverage and a wellness plan with incentives for participating in preventive activities such as annual physicals. The new plan also required mandatory newborn critical and congenital heart disease screening and vision screenings for every school-aged child before kindergarten and before third grade.

In 2016, the Legislature created ABLE (Achieving a Better Life Experience) Accounts that allow individuals with disabilities to save money for future living or education expenses, without impacting eligibility for Medicaid or Social Security. The accounts, which are similar to college savings plans, allow individuals to save up to $15,000 annually and up to $100,000 total.

League lobbying in 2017 defeated a Medicaid work requirement and succeeded in promoting legislation requiring stronger government oversight of the privatized Medicaid system, including specific benchmarks and standards expected. And the passage of HF 758 in 2019 expanded access to Medicaid for pregnant women who have legal protected status —those who are in the five-year waiting period for citizenship.

Signature Legislation

Juvenile justice: The League began studying issues surrounding justice for juveniles in the late 1930s, and has adopted and expanded positions since then. Currently, the LWVIA supports a community approach to the prevention of juvenile delinquent behavior by advocating the use of public and private resources to encourage the development of healthy and nurturing families; assure safety for children in their communities; facilitate the positive attachment of children to their families and their schools/education; encourage children in the formation of positive peer relations; reward children's justice principles whenever possible; establish and adequately fund a variety of treatment options to address children's underlying or contributing problems; encourage coordination among treatment agencies; and incorporate restorative justice principles whenever possible.

Legislation passed in 1967 closed juvenile court proceedings to the press, with a decision otherwise left to the judge's discretion. In 1975, the Legislature determined that only criminal offenses could be considered delinquent acts, and delinquency must be proved beyond a reasonable doubt.

In 1976, Senator Minnette Doderer and Representative Joan Lipsky teamed up to develop a package of juvenile justice reforms under the guidance of University of Iowa law professor Josephine Gittler. One of the objectives was to codify all juvenile laws into one chapter of the Iowa Code to guide lawyers, judges, social workers, and others dealing with children. Iowa laws also needed to reflect recent U.S. Supreme Court decisions about juvenile offenders. And, drafters of this juvenile justice package wanted children to be treated in the least restrictive manner and given as much responsibility for themselves as possible. Opponents viewed many of the reforms as controversial shifts from previously accepted norms. Examples included decriminalizing running away from home, which was not an illegal act for an adult. Related to that issue was the removal of skipping school and incorrigibility as status offenses. Despite opposition, the juvenile justice reform package passed in 1978 with these provisions, as well as one that stipulated that a child who had not committed a crime could not be held in detention longer than a child who had.

HF 1048, passed in 1976, prohibited jailing juveniles for traffic offenses. And SF 515, passed in 1997, authorized peer review courts and was codified in Code 602.6110.

In 1982, Senator Doderer helped secure legislation that, in cases of incest, allowed the court to remove the offending adult from the home, rather than the child, to better ensure the child's safety. After Senator Doderer's tenure in the Iowa Legislature ended, the League Justice Committee continued work on reforms, such as a 1994 law that required school dropouts to return to school or training of some kind to obtain a driver's license.

The League's work on behalf of juveniles has been applauded by many across the years, including George Belitsos, Youth Shelter Services, in 1996: "The League has had a huge role in the Juvenile Justice Code under which we now operate." Jo Ann Finkenbinder, Black Hawk-Bremer League, is an example of a dedicated League member with an interest in criminal and juvenile justice. She was selected for a two-year appointment beginning in 2017 to represent the state League on the Iowa Department of Human Rights Criminal and Juvenile Justice Planning Team's SMART on Juvenile Justice Planning Initiative. Iowa received a $270,800 grant to develop a data-driven juvenile justice strategic plan. The plan is to include recommendations to improve public safety and outcomes for youth, their families, and the communities in which they live. It also will detail how the state will reinvest the savings realized through reduced use of placing youth out of their homes and increased use of effective alternatives to out-of-home placement to ensure reform efforts are sustained.

The League's work for juveniles continued with support for legislation in 2017 that provided diversion options for juveniles who committed delinquent acts, with their records sealed upon successful completion. And in 2019, SF 589 added five years to the statute of limitations for sexual assault of a minor by a therapist, counselor, or school employee. SF 615 included new funding for juvenile delinquency prevention in cities that have populations greater than eighty thousand and a higher-than-normal rate of juvenile crime.

Mental Health

LWVIA's current position calls for a coordinated, comprehensive, and adequately state-funded delivery system that ensures convenient and equitable access to an established menu of mental health services; early detection and treatment of mental illnesses and co-occurring abuse disorders with efficient, effective, and evidence-based programs and services; individualization of care to meet people's needs in or near their home communities; and eradication of the stigma of mental illness.

The General Assembly first passed appropriations for mental health facilities in 1945 and 1947. During those same years, the League began studying mental health and advocating for improved services, an example again of the League being "ahead of the game" in regard to the needs of our state's vulnerable citizens. The 1958 convention program listed these needed changes: establish an Iowa Department of Mental Health; revise commitment laws; provide for follow-up evaluation of treatment effectiveness; provide for a Citizen's Committee to assist the director of Mental Health in implementing an up-to-date program, as well as distribute information and arouse civilian interest in problems of mental health (we now call that transparency); and pass legislation to provide state aid to medical students in order to enhance entry into psychiatry and a career in Iowa (a recommendation that took fifty years to be adopted).

In 1950, the Legislature revised Iowa Code Chapter 229 Commitment and Discharge to allow any citizen to make a voluntary personal application for admission to a state hospital for the purpose of securing observation, examination, diagnosis, and treatment for mental illness. And 1951 witnessed the passage of legislation that allowed residents to voluntarily apply for admission to one of the state's mental health institutions for the treatment of alcoholism.

In 1965, the Legislature created a state committee on mental hygiene and its composition and functioning. The committee was written into the Code in 1966 under Chapter 225B.1–7 Iowa Code for the Mental Health Authority. This action by the Iowa Legislature was in order to comply with the benefits of U.S. Public Law 487.

The passage in 1975 of HF 390 allowed county boards to spend federal funds for mental health centers or programs for mentally disabled individuals without referendums. And legislation passed in 1994 established grants to communities for development of local, tailored mental health programs.

In 2005, legislation required mental health parity in insurance coverage offered by businesses with fifty or more employees. However, it mandated coverage only for biologically based mental illnesses and not for substance abuse or problems affecting children, such as eating disorders.

The years 2012–13 saw a three-phase redesign of portions of the state's mental health delivery system. In 2012, the first part of this process involved mandating core services, setting target populations, and establishing a system of governance. Phase two and three followed, when the Legislature regionalized local mental health and disability services, fixing the system's funding. In 2013, the state took over responsibility for paying the non-federal share of Medicaid, called the Medicaid lift, and implemented a plan for "full funding."

In 2017, the Legislature mandated annual suicide prevention training for school employees and teachers. Lawmakers also passed legislation that encouraged the development of an array of integrated mental health, disability, and substance use disorder services for individuals with complex issues, as well as stabilized the funding.

The 2018 HF 766 bill allowed service regions to use other county funds to backfill any shortfall. In the same General Assembly session, HF 2456 passed to establish myriad regulations for mental health services in the state, labeled Mental Health Complex Needs.

HF 690, passed in 2019, established a regionally managed children's mental health system with new core services available to children diagnosed with serious emotional disturbances and new core crisis services available to children with any condition. The legislation also added family members of children served, educators, and children's service providers as members of the regional governing boards and codified the Governor's Children's Behavioral Health State Board. The new law required regions to pay for services to families who do not have Medicaid or private insurance, at a level up to 500 percent of the federal poverty level. It also stipulated that Medicaid include coverage for these services within managed care contracts. However, no state funds were identified for these services, and provision of the services was guaranteed only to the extent funding was available. But regions can maintain up to 40 percent of their budgets in reserve until July 1, 2023, to help pay for the development of the new children's services.

Poverty

To reduce or prevent poverty, the League supports policies and programs designed to increase job opportunities; increase access to health insurance; provide support services such as childcare and transportation; provide opportunities and/or incentives for basic or remedial education and job training; decrease teen pregnancy; and ensure that non-custodial parents contribute to the support of their children.

1943 saw the creation of the first Iowa program for Aid to Dependent Children (ADC). The federal Social Security Act of 1935 established the ADC program to provide financial assistance to needy dependent children with state participation voluntary. Once a state's ADC plan was approved by federal administrators, the state received reimbursement from the federal government for a portion of state funds expended for needy children. In 1946, the Iowa Code included a new section, Chapter 239.1-18 Aid to Dependent Children. The League has consistently worked for expansion and adequate funding of welfare programs, such as early intervention and preschool programs, health care coverage, and childcare assistance. The League has also monitored the administration of ADC. In the 1980s, when benefits were being cut to women with dependent children if a man might be living in the home, changes were made to DHS policy on what constituted a qualifying family. The name of the program changed to Aid to Families with Dependent Children (AFDC).

Legislation passed in 1975 created a new legal designation for use by the courts and Social Services: "Child in Need of Assistance" (CINA). Codified in Code 232.2(6), a CINA is defined as an unmarried child whose parent or guardian had abandoned, abused, neglected him/her, or denied her/him needed care. The term is still in use today.

Health care for low-income individuals also is a concern of the League. Before 1986, the University of Iowa Hospitals and Clinics provided medical care for indigent individuals, primarily pregnant women receiving welfare benefits. This necessitated travel to Iowa City, generally one or more weeks ahead of the expected delivery. This practice placed a burden not only on patients but also on their families due to long absences from home. The university hospital supported this centralized approach because it provided training opportunities for medical students. A group of female legislators, several of them League members, wrote and floor-managed a bill to decentralize health care for pregnant women and others receiving welfare benefits. Passage of the bill allowed them to receive such care in their local communities.

Meeting basic needs of those with incomes at or near the poverty level also is a League concern. During the 1990s, the Legislature created Iowa's Emergency Assistance Program (EAP), which used state and federal matching funds to provide up to $500 per year to families with children under the age of eighteen. The money could be used to pay for rent, utilities, and purchase or repair of heating equipment. And in 1994, legislation established breakfast programs in schools with more than 35 percent of students qualifying for free or reduced-price lunches.

In 2019, the League helped to stall legislation requiring Iowans receiving public assistance to work or do some type of community engagement (SF 334). Also that year, HF 766 made changes in Department of Human Services funding to begin alignment with new federal Family First legislation. These changes included adding twenty-nine caseworkers, expanding core services, and merging funding for group foster care, child welfare emergency services, shelter care, and other allocations, which allowed for more flexibility in meeting needs. In addition, SF 2418 Medicaid Oversight passed, establishing guidelines for the provision of services. Medicaid issues frequently arise in the Legislature due to funding of such services, as well as federal changes in reimbursement. So the League has been and will continue to be involved in monitoring this large government expenditure.

Senior Care

The current population growth of people ages sixty-five and older is one of the most significant demographic trends in U.S. history. Baby boomers—those born between 1946 and 1964 and thus ages fifty-six to seventy-four in 2020—have brought both challenges and opportunities to the economy, infrastructure, and institutions as they have passed through each major stage of life. Although U.S. policymakers and others have had many decades to plan for the inevitable aging of the baby boom cohort, it is not clear that sufficient preparations have been made to meet baby boomers' anticipated needs in old age. By 2030, when all surviving baby boomers will be over sixty-five, they will number seventy-two million—20 percent of the U.S. population. Here is some Iowa legislation to begin to address the needs of our current elderly citizens and the large number who will join them in the foreseeable future.

HF 2275, passed in 1998, required nursing homes and employers of in-home health care workers to conduct criminal background checks on all prospective employees. It also mandated monthly nursing home report cards on their compliance with state regulations.

Killing a bill can be as important as passing a bill! For example, in 1999, SF 300 would have undermined both state and consumer efforts to ensure the safety of Iowa's nursing home residents by not making nursing home violations public information. And if a deficiency or problem were corrected, it would be expunged from the record so the public would not see any history of non-compliance. The League and others lobbied successfully for the bill's defeat.

In 2000, SF 2193 Senior Living Program/Trust Fund provided funds to convert nursing homes to assisted living and other long-term care alternatives for lower- and middle-income seniors; expand home health care services for this same demographic; develop facilities that offer adult day care, special needs childcare, and respite care services; and provide Iowans with information about long-term care services in their communities, Medicaid availability for seniors, and planning for care in one's senior years. The Legislature earmarked $82 million for the fund, and the federal Health Care Financing Administration granted an additional $270 million for this long-term care system. The floor manager for the bill's passage was Leaguer and legislator Mona Martin of Davenport.

Other Legislation

ONLY IN A RURAL STATE LIKE IOWA!

In 1953, the Legislature was the site of Nelson's Margarine War. Gladys Nelson of Jasper County served in the Iowa Legislature from 1951 to 1957. In 1953, Mrs. Nelson took up the issue of Iowa women's concerns about restrictions on margarine sales. The state's Dairy Association and the Farm Bureau opposed the production and sale of newly produced margarine, which drove down butter sales. These organizations successfully lobbied the Legislature to place a nickel tax on margarine and to ban the sale of colored margarine, even though no studies had found margarine to be harmful and many households welcomed a lower-cost alternative to butter. Because many consumers found white margarine unappealing, margarine producers sold packets of yellow dye with their product, which homemakers had to mix in by hand to achieve a more acceptable spread.

Mrs. Nelson, the only woman in the Legislature at the time, decided to advocate for women who resented the time and effort required to make white margarine "look like butter." She had support from border county grocers who were losing millions of dollars a year in sales when shoppers crossed state lines to purchase colored margarine in neighboring states and bought other groceries while there. Iowa also lost sales tax revenue from out-of-state grocery shopping. Knowing her male colleagues were unfamiliar with the hands-on practice of coloring margarine, Nelson organized a group of housewives to attend a committee meeting with margarine containers and yellow dye in hand to demonstrate the time-consuming and messy process. At one point during the debates, the House passed an amendment that required margarine to be packaged in a triangular shape to alert customers they were not buying butter, despite the fact that no equipment was yet available to make a triangular package. Nelson was quick to tell the Farm Bureau lobbyist who promoted the amendment: "... you have sold your prestige as a great state organization down the river for a mess of rancid butter ...".

Confronting the dairy industry and the Farm Bureau could have been political suicide. But Representative Nelson, who floor-managed the bill, by the end of the session had won repeal of the tax and approval for the legal sale of colored margarine in any shape. And she won the election for another term In the House! Mrs. Nelson was a longtime mentor of League members in Iowa.

WHO PAYS AND FOR WHAT?

The League has always been concerned about "the best bang for your buck," or fiscal responsibility in government, but also recognized that other factors need consideration. In 1967, the League took up the issue of where abandoned children born at the University of Iowa hospital or the children of veterans who could not support them would receive care. At the time, these children lived at the Annie Wittenmyer Home in Davenport, with the state paying one hundred percent of the cost of their care. One obstacle to placing these children in foster care in their home communities, a more appropriate placement for their growth and development, was that the county of residence would have to assume the cost of foster care. Representative Joan Lipsky of Cedar Rapids, a psychologist, sponsored a bill to change that policy so the state would pay one hundred percent for foster care, as it did for care at the Wittenmyer Home.

CHANGE IN ATTITUDES AND ACTIONS REGARDING ALCOHOL USE BY YOUTH

In regard to the protection of children on certain issues, legislators have been divided in their views and have vacillated across time. One example is the purchase of alcohol. After a federal constitutional amendment lowered the age for voting to eighteen in 1971, the Iowa Legislature debated the age at which one should be able to buy or be served alcoholic beverages. The "ping pong game" began in 1972, when the Legislature lowered the drinking age from twenty-one to nineteen. A year later, after considerable debate, the age was lowered to eighteen. Because of public and political pressure in the intervening years, the Legislature raised the legal drinking age back to nineteen in 1978. Then, when the federal government tied certain funding to states to the legal alcohol purchase and possession age, it was raised to twenty-one. (Note: The League did not have a position on this issue, but several legislators leading the proposed bills were League members.)

CHILD SAFETY A MUST

Jean Lloyd-Jones's Buckle Up Baby bill passed in 1985, making car travel safer for babies and toddlers. Children under the age of two had to be buckled into an approved child safety seat, and those ages two to four had to be in an approved safety seat or buckled with a seat belt. Thirty-five years later, the seats are safer, and state regulations have been continually refined. As of March 2019, children under one and less than twenty pounds need a rear-facing approved child safety seat; ages one to six need a child restraint system, such as a car seat or booster seat; and ages six to eighteen need a child restraint system or a seat belt.

The late 1980s saw another child safety bill, but for a bit older age group. Janet Adams, of Hamilton County and former League president, heard from a middle school classmate of one of her seven children that riding a moped was not safe if drivers couldn't see it. So, Representative Adams introduced and managed passage of a bill requiring orange flags on mopeds as visual markers of the vehicles and their riders. Currently, a moped must be equipped with a day glow orange safety flag that extends no less than five feet above the ground and is attached to the rear of the moped; it must be triangular in shape with a surface area no less than thirty square inches. So, legislators, listen to your constituents, no matter how young they are!

COLLABORATION AND PROBLEM-SOLVING GO A LONG WAY

Representative Lloyd-Jones of Iowa City helped in the late 1970s establish the Women's Caucus, consisting of female legislators from both political parties. Initially, the caucus convened at dinner meetings away from the Capitol. The caucus not only helped reduce the isolation of female legislators, but also provided an avenue for networking and finding support for common causes that could result in proposed legislation. The group was not just interested in children, education, marriage and divorce, and equal rights for women—what their male counterparts might label "women's issues"—but also topics such as prison reform, land use, water quality, and government fiscal responsibility. Another self-selected task the Women's Caucus assumed was the instruction and nurturing of the young female pages and other female staffers at the Capitol, particularly in the area of sexual harassment. This was long before the issue was discussed publicly or policies were developed to deal with it. The female legislators defined sexual harassment for these young employees and provided guidance on what to do if it occurred. These legislators also took it upon themselves to informally intercede with any male who exhibited harassing behavior.

II. Education Legislation: Education Leads to Participation

The roots of the League's commitment to education began in the suffrage movement. Many suffragists were educators. Mary Shelton Huston of Burlington fought for equal pay with male teachers who were less well-educated, while Laetitia Conard taught at Grinnell College with no monetary compensation. Other Iowa women who worked for suffrage also were teachers: Arabella Babb Mansfield, Rowena Edson Stevens, and Vivian Smith (see Chapter 2 Appendix). And League founder Carrie Chapman Catt was a school superintendent, so teaching was important to her. Her belief in education led to her commitment to training people to be informed voters, even developing the citizenship curriculum mentioned in Chapter 5. Thus, it is understandable that education would be and has been one of the League's highest priorities. Its lobbying efforts have been guided by several key tenets. One is that every child should have access to a free public education within a system that provides equal opportunity for all. Another is that efficient and economical government requires competent personnel, a clear assignment of responsibility, adequate financing, and coordination among the different agencies and levels of government.

At the time of the League's establishment, Iowa already mandated compulsory education for children ages seven to sixteen. But over the years, the League has identified numerous other issues and promoted legislation to correct problems, in areas such as equalization of educational opportunities, financing of public education, and administration of schools.

Free Public Education for All

Vocational education: In 1921, legislation was passed to accept a federal act to provide for the promotion of vocational rehabilitation of people disabled in industry or otherwise and their return to civil employment. The legislation established a state agency to administer such a program (previous legislation establishing evening schools for adults had passed in 1917).

Special education services: In 1946, a director of special education position (Chapter 281) was created in the Department of Public Instruction. Certain students not already served in state special schools were identified by statute for services within school districts or by cooperating districts: blind, deaf, and speech-impaired students as well as students with impaired health due to tuberculosis, heart disease, or other physical disabilities. Thanks to the diligence of Representative Joan Lipsky of Cedar Rapids, the Legislature in 1969 mandated special remedial reading and speech and language services for students in need, as well as other services for deaf and blind children.

Iowa also led the nation in creating more efficient educational delivery structures. In 1974, the Legislature passed a bill establishing fifteen Area Education Agencies (AEAs) (now nine such regions) to provide services and programs requested by local school districts, along with required special education support. The League study of this delivery system yielded the following 1979 position on AEAs, emphasizing funding and efficiency of services provided, and specifying that they should "… have no regulatory or taxing powers; give assistance to local school districts for talented and gifted programs, preferably funded through a weighted enrollment formula; not duplicate programs and services already available through other school corporations in the state; and be funded through a combination of property taxes, state aid, and grants."

English as a Second Language (ESL): In 2002, a bill providing an additional $1.2 million for ESL classes for schoolchildren passed, with the funding available the following school year. In 2019, the Legislature appropriated new funding of $500,000, via HF 766, for community colleges to assist students with ESL, and continued $200,000 in funding for Refugee RISE (Rebuild Integrate Serve Empower) and $210,000 for refugee integration.

Higher education: In 1909, the state established the State Board of Education to oversee, coordinate, and govern Iowa's three public universities, the Iowa School for the Deaf, and the Iowa Braille and Sight Saving School. The name was changed in 1955 to the State Board of Regents. In 1962, legislation (Chapter 262) authorized the board to construct buildings and facilities for the comfort, convenience, and welfare of students—such as student unions, recreational buildings, auditoriums, stadiums, field houses, athletic buildings, and parking areas. The cost of such construction was to be paid by student fees and charges for use.

In regard to the cost of post-secondary education at the Regents' institutions, the League has consistently worked for state higher education funding. The organization's 1957 position is still relevant today: "Increased appropriations for operating expenses at the state institutions of higher education are required because of … 1) increasing demands in a great number of areas for professional persons with advanced and highly technical training and 2) demands from the public or pressure of events to establish new curriculum programs or strengthen existing ones."

Early childhood education: The League was one of the first groups in Iowa to access, along with educators, the research on the benefits of early childhood education—particularly for those three- to five-year-old children who do not attend a private preschool due to their family's lack of ability to pay. The Community Empowerment legislation of 1998 provided funding for a variety of coordinated services for children five and younger, including funding for free preschool for children in families below a certain income level.

By 2000, the empowerment funds for Iowa communities had grown to $15.6 million, including school readiness dollars for children five and younger. Many preschool programs established through the empowerment grants have been absorbed by the school districts where they originated, with continued funding by the district based on the improvement in kindergarten and first grade achievement evidenced by the "empowered preschoolers."

School vouchers: The League has a twenty-plus-year history of opposing tuition tax credits (or vouchers), and in 2017 and 2018 helped to defeat bills that would have allowed school vouchers for children attending non-public schools. The League position: "Public schools are the very foundation of our strong, democratic society, providing services to all children regardless of ethnic background, socioeconomic status, special needs, or religious beliefs. An equitable and stable tax base policy allows government to provide valuable services, like public education, in the most efficient and economical manner. Offering tuition tax credits would take resources from other needed programs."

Human growth and development: In the words of former state League president and former legislator Jane Teaford (Black Hawk-Bremer League): "Prior to a 1988 bill, in 1987, the Legislature passed SF 2094 that set up a state task force on adolescent pregnancy, mandated a human growth and development curriculum in all K-12 school districts, and established an Adolescent Pregnancy Prevention Grant program that the governor vetoed. The Adolescent Pregnancy Prevention Grant program, however, was funded and began operation in October 1987. The governor then appointed a Governor's Task Force on Adolescence. In August 1987, this task force began to address the issues of adolescent pregnancy, substance abuse, and teen suicide and began to identify resources available to combat the problems. At the same time, the Legislative Study Committee on Adolescence was established to examine the problems. The recommendations from these groups included a K-12 human growth and development curriculum. We didn't dare talk about sex education or anything very specific, and we couldn't pass if it required schools to actually use the curriculum. However, an excellent Human Growth and Development Curriculum Guide was developed and made available to all public schools. Part of the curriculum did address pregnancy prevention. I have been told that the curriculum was wonderful and very useful."

In 2018, the League was successful in defeating HF 2162, which would have limited Title X federal funding to non-abortion providers for family planning and sex education.

Iowa League of Women Voters *Broadside No. 6* from March 1943 in support of HF 300.

Financing Public Education

Using statewide distribution of the flyer above, the League worked diligently for the 1943 passage of the massive (437 pages with eleven articles) HF 300 bill. The bill passed after some rewriting for clarification and consistency with other laws. In 1946, the Legislature passed legislation authorizing state aid to districts for transportation costs per a reimbursement schedule (Chapter 285), as well as supplemental aid for educational programming under certain conditions and requirements (Chapter 286).

League Study Committees, as well as volunteer and paid lobbyists, have spent much time across the decades monitoring public K-12 education funding. This interest initially arose from the use of property taxes alone to fund public school education. The League's position was that such a funding mechanism led to inequality of educational opportunity due to variations in property values across the state. This position, bolstered with data the League had gathered on the wide discrepancies in expenditures in the state's school districts, led the League to lobby for change in the late 1960s. The League's work paid off in 1971 with the passage of the School Foundation Program. This law based state aid on school district enrollment, with a substantial increase in aid to each district.

Another statewide League study in the late 1980s yielded the following position on school finance: "State aid should constitute a higher proportion of the controlled budget than property taxes; districts should be allowed to supplement their general budgets above the state-controlled level; regular re-calculation of the state cost per pupil aid should occur; and allowable growth for districts should be based on a combination of factors."

Signature Legislation

Lobbying legislators based on the League's school finance position, the organization helped gain passage of the 1989 retooling of the **Iowa Code** (**Chapter 257**), with implementation in 1992. This school finance legislation (HF 535) provided avenues for achieving greater equity for Iowa students: increased state aid for low-spending districts; extra funding for meeting the needs of students with special needs, i.e. a weighted per-pupil schedule for special education students and gifted students; and at-risk and early childhood program funding.

Iowa Code Chapter 257 essentially has remained the school finance approach for nearly thirty years, with regular legislative decision-making related to: the school aid formula; the use of federal funds, such as those from the American Recovery and Reinvestment Act (ARRA) Education Fiscal Stabilization (2009); the addition of provisions to assist school districts in maintaining fiscal responsibility (state sales/use tax allowable for school infrastructure in 2008); and the addition of new program funding, such as that for dropout prevention (2009–15)—all supported by the League.

School organization and administration

Pension plans: School boards had been able to establish pension and annuity retirement systems for public school teachers since 1917. In 1931, the population limit for districts offering such a benefit dropped from seventy-five thousand or more to twenty-five thousand, with ratification by popular vote for districts with populations between twenty-five thousand and seventy-five thousand. In 1953, the Iowa Public Employees' Retirement System (Chapter 97B) replaced the Iowa Old-Age and Survivors' System, which had replaced individual school district pension and annuity plans for teachers.

Textbook charges to students: Before 1937, the state only authorized school districts to sell textbooks to students at cost. In 1937, the Legislature passed a law (Code 4446 Adoption-Purchase and Sale) allowing school boards to loan textbooks to students free of charge. In 1939, additional legislation allowed districts to rent textbooks to students.

Wages for public school teachers: In 1939, the minimum wage (Chapter 223) was set at not less than $50 per month, with no constraints on districts that chose to pay more. In 1946, teacher monthly pay was differentiated (Chapter 294.6) by the type of teaching certificate held and number of college credits earned, ranging from $70 per month for a valid teaching certificate to $90 per month for a limited elementary certificate based on sixty or more hours of college credits earned. The Iowa Code on wages continued to allow for higher monthly wages at a district's discretion.

Educational administration: In 1946, to encourage consolidation, the Legislature passed laws (Chapters 273 and 275) that allowed for the creation of county school districts, with elected boards of education having powers over policy, finance, and appointment of superintendents (Chapter 271). In 1950, additional legislation specified greater refinement of the functions of county school districts. Consolidation legislation reflected the League position on government efficiency because there were 4,652 school districts in Iowa at that time! In 1957, legislation passed that permitted a school superintendent to serve more than one school district. Joint county school districts were allowed in 1965 (when there were just 1,098 school districts), as part of a continuing effort for a more efficient educational delivery system. Such reorganization eventually did reduce the number of Iowa school districts to 384 by 1995 (367 in 2019–2020).

The League continues to collect data on educational services across the state and lobby for identified needs or changes. Universal preschool with appropriate funding is an issue the League will continue to support, as well as the coordination of services between the Department of Education and other agencies dealing with children, such as human services, the judicial branch, and public health.

III. Environment Legislation: Saving the Planet

Since the 1960s, the League of Women Voters of the United States has been at the forefront of efforts to protect air, land, and water resources after thorough study and development of this position: "… support … the preservation of the physical, chemical, and biological integrity of the ecosystem and … maximum protection of public health and the environment, … use a problem-solving approach to environmental protection and pollution control, … attend to the interrelationships of air, water, and land resources when designing environmental safeguards, … and aim for the prevention of ecological degradation and the reduction and control of pollutants before they go down the sewer, up the chimney, or into the landfill."

After passage at the federal level of the Clean Air (1970 and 1990), Clean Water (1987), Safe Drinking Water (1987), Resource Conservation and Recovery (hazardous waste management), and Toxic Substance Control (1976) acts, the national League has worked continually for effective regulatory programs related to these laws. State and local Leagues have gathered data on the results of implementation of these laws in their locales. The national League has fought against attempts across time to weaken these federal laws, and state and local Leagues have worked for adherence to the laws and increased funding to address issues in their communities.

Frank Miller cartoon from July 3, 1975. "I know what's causing this air stagnation! It's that danged new Celsius system!" Permission granted by the *Des Moines Register*.

Air

A 1993 bill established that the state would administer the federal Clean Air Act, which the League had been lobbying for since the 1990 revision of the act. The League was not pleased with the bare minimum funding included in the bill, nor with the fact that it did not reinstate the program that until 1991 had regulated more than sixty air toxins in Iowa.

Energy

1975 legislation included SF 289, which provided $1 million to the Energy Policy Council for research and development, and SF 419, which allowed the Department of Environmental Quality and Energy Policy Council to advise if requested by a city, county, or private agency operating a sanitary disposal system.

A major piece of League-supported legislation aimed at reduction of litter and conservation of energy and natural resources, a law that has impacted most of us living in Iowa since the late 1970s, is known as the bottle bill. The **Renewable Beverage Container Act** of 1978 became effective in 1979. Representative Mary O'Halloran of Black Hawk County worked with many colleagues for the passage of this bill, which also was supported by then-Governor Robert Ray (see Chapter 6).

Within one year of the law taking effect, the Iowa Department of Transportation reported a 79 percent drop in bottle and can litter and a 38 percent reduction in overall roadside litter. Levels of litter on Iowa highways remain low compared to other states. And 2012 data, provided by redemption centers around the state that emerged after the passage of this bill, revealed that 92 percent of glass bottles, 88 percent of aluminum cans, and 76 percent of carbonated bottles are recovered from this recycling effort.

Iowa continues to have one of the highest can and bottle redemption rates in the nation, a rate nearly three times that of non-deposit states. 2017 survey results showed that 88 percent of Iowans had a favorable view of the bottle bill and thought it had been good for the state, with similar percentage levels across all political party affiliations.

The League has been watchful (some say "watch dogging") of bills introduced in the Legislature to repeal this forty-year-old law that has had such a dramatic impact on litter and recycling. In 2017, 2018, and 2019, the League and its collaborators succeeded in defeating attempts to weaken or eliminate it. Those collaborators will continue to defend this law as well as work for bottle bill improvements, such as expanding the legislation to include sports drinks and water bottles, increasing the deposit to ten cents, and increasing the handling fee for grocers and redemption centers to better cover their costs.

Other Energy Legislation

The goal behind HF 753, the Waste Volume Reduction and Recycling Act (1989), was a significant reduction in the type and amount of waste going into landfills beginning in 1991. The law banned waste oil, lead acid batteries, and some kinds of food products and beverage containers. The bill also required state agencies to have recycling programs and to begin to purchase a certain percentage of recycled paper.

In 1990, the League supported an energy efficiency bill, SF 2403. It was very comprehensive in scope, with these highlights: developed programs to reduce Iowa's dependence on imported energy; required public buildings to consider lifecycle costs; required municipal utilities and rural electric cooperatives to file energy efficiency plans; incorporated federal fuel economy standards for automobiles in the state fleet; required rate-related gas utilities to dedicate 1.5 percent of their gross revenues to energy efficiency programs such as giving away water heater blankets; and required rate-related electric utilities to dedicate 2 percent of their gross revenues to energy efficiency programs.

In 1991, regulations for medical waste disposal were added to the Waste Volume Reduction and Recycling Act of 1989. The League was involved in following proposed bills in 1999–2001 for the regulation of power plants and the location of new ones.

Land Use

Former LWVIA President Jean Lloyd-Jones: "The League is always ahead of the game, and we coined the term 'land use' here in Iowa in the early 1970s." To help legislators and the public understand the term and its components, the League organized, with an Interim Legislative Study Committee, a two-day conference in Des Moines in 1972 with a nationally known land use specialist. Five regional follow-up meetings were held around the state. It's the League Way—inform yourselves, then others, and lead the way for needed change.

The League of Women Voters of Iowa subsequently developed its land use position in 1973 for use in advocacy by local Leagues and lobbying by the state League: "… integrated local, county, regional, and state land use policy which enhances quality of life and provides for preservation of prime agricultural land and sensitive natural areas, … soil and water conservation, … managed urban growth which protects agricultural land, fosters higher density urban development, encourages infill development and re-development in cities, and preserves natural areas, … a statewide land capability inventory, … a diversified transportation system, … [and] statewide distribution of natural areas, open spaces, and public recreation areas …"

Legislation impacting land practices began with the Fertilizer and Pesticide Review Board that was created in 1970 via HF 1198. Then, the Soil Conservancy Act passed in 1973. 1975 was a banner year for environmental legislation, most of it regarding land use. For example, the Legislature passed HF 736, which required carriers of hazardous waste to notify police if they were involved in an accident. SF 314 created new regulations for strip mining operations, such as requiring re-vegetation and imposing fees and other penalties for non-compliance. However, not all environmental legislation proposed in 1975 was successful. HF 505, which would have created a state Land Use Policy Commission, passed in the House but failed to make it out of the Senate. The 1975 push for new environmental protections was led by Representative Mary O'Halloran of Cedar Falls (Black Hawk-Bremer League), who served in the Iowa House from 1972 to 1978. After her service in the Iowa Legislature, Representative O'Halloran assumed a position with the federal Department of Energy.

After six years of League work, the Legislature passed HF 210 in 1977, setting up the mechanism for the Temporary County and State Land Preservation Policy Commission charged with recommending a land use policy to the Legislature and a method of implementing it. All ninety-nine counties researched their county's situation, held public hearings for information and citizen input, and determined criteria for land use regulation, which were submitted for consideration for the final legislation. More than eight thousand Iowans participated in this process.

1979 saw the establishment of a Solid Waste Disposal Commission within the Department of Environmental Quality, with the task of developing a comprehensive plan for state management of hazardous waste under federal guidelines. The Legislature passed HF 2561 in 1980, setting up an interagency coordinating committee under the State Soil Conservation Committee to make recommendations for dealing with water management problems affecting more than one state and thus agency jurisdictions. An example of such an issue is soil erosion due to the annual loss of ten tons of soil per acre from sloping fields.

The League also supported the federal Superfund for Hazardous Waste, formally known as the Comprehensive Environmental Response, Compensation, and Liability Act of 1980. The purpose of the superfund is to identify sites where hazardous materials threaten the environment and then oversee actions needed to mitigate or eliminate, if possible, the polluting or contaminating materials. The superfund attempts to compel responsible parties, when they can be identified, to fund cleanup activities. Historically, about 70 percent of contamination mitigation costs have been paid by parties deemed responsible, with the remainder financed by tax dollars. As of August 16, 2019, the U.S. Environmental Protection Agency's website lists 1,343 locations classified as National Priorities List (NPL) sites, with 414 former NPL sites designated as "deleted," or no longer a threat to public health. Twelve current and ten deleted NPL sites are in Iowa. In that same vein, in 1984 the League supported HF 2099, which dealt with the handling and disposal of hazardous substances.

The League, along with others*, worked for the passage in 1989 of legislation to establish the Resource Enhancement and Protection (REAP) program in Iowa. Over the last thirty years, the League has monitored the program's administration and funding levels. The program received $12 million in 2019, though $1 million was siphoned off for state park operations, and any unused REAP funds will go to pay for flood repair in parks. Funding for trails within REAP was increased by $500,000, bringing the total funds allocated to $1.5 million. [*Originally twenty-five private conservation-related organizations, there now are thirty-eight different partners, including recreation, conservation, historical preservation, and sporting organizations, working to fund public land acquisition, historic preservation, cost-sharing programs with farmers to enhance water quality and soil conservation, community projects, and conservation education.]

In 1991, the League worked on the Recycling and Waste Reduction bill that promoted policies dealing with the recycling of household hazardous waste, including safe treatment, storage, and disposal.

Water Quality

In 1965, through HF 412, the Legislature established a Water Pollution Control Commission. By 1970, the League was concerned about the functioning of the commission and recommended to the Legislature several changes to the administrative structure of Iowa's agencies involved in control of water pollution. Eight organizations joined the League in making recommendations for a reorganization bill, SF 666, which subsequently created a Department of Natural Resources Management.

In 1975, the League supported SF 2, which prohibited underground gas storage tanks within city limits. The bill passed in the Senate but not in the House. The League was still promoting in 1987 the passage of stringent underground storage tank rules in HF 643. The following year, HF 2441 established a state-administered insurance fund to cover repair of damage from leaking tanks. The fund would cover up to $500,000 of cleanup costs.

That same year, the League worked for passage of the Iowa Groundwater Protection bill (HF 631), which provided for education, research, and demonstration projects; placed restrictions on use of agricultural chemicals; levied fees on the sale of pesticides and nitrogen fertilizers; and provided funding for the Leopold Center at Iowa State and the Iowa Hygienic Lab. Also in 1988, the Legislature passed a tough law that would force those responsible to pay for pollution cleanup, with fines starting at $25,000 a day and possible jail terms.

An Agricultural Drainage Well bill in 1997 authorized the Department of Agriculture to pay up to 75 percent of a landowner's costs for establishing an alternative drainage system on land where that landowner must close drainage wells. The bill also established a funding stream to support the program.

In 2002, the League worked to limit the amount of manure that could be spread on agricultural land, depending on phosphorous levels, as a way to improve water quality. The Livestock Confinement Bill also prohibited confinement operations in a one-hundred-year floodplain, and it mandated that construction permits for confinement buildings could allow space for only 2,600 hogs rather than 4,100, resulting in smaller confinement units.

The League in 2006 fought against construction of livestock confinement operations in vulnerable areas where pollution of ground or surface water could occur, as well as worked to bring Iowa into compliance with the U.S. Clean Water Act. In 2008, the League helped secure the passage of legislation requiring septic tanks to be inspected when property is sold to ensure that they are not leaking sewage into lakes, streams, and underground water. If found defective, the property owner must make repairs before the sale can be completed.

2009 found the League working to prevent future flooding in Iowa by requiring better land management. That year, the Legislature passed the Surface Water Protection and Flood Mitigation Act (HF 756), which provided for the management of watersheds by two bodies: the Watershed Improvement Review Board and the Water Resources Coordinating Council. The act tasked the council with preserving and protecting Iowa's water resources and coordinating the management of those resources in a sustainable and fiscally responsible manner. In addition, the law required the council to develop recommendations for policies and funding to reduce the adverse impact of future flooding.

In 2015, the Legislature more than doubled funding for water quality (from $4.4 million to $9.6 million) with support for the creation of a three-year pilot project to collect in-field practices data. That data would be used to track progress in reducing nutrient flow to watersheds in Iowa from non-point sources, as identified in the Iowa Nutrient Reduction Strategy. The League supported the legislation but advocated for public reporting, which was not included. But the League was pleased in 2017 when the data from the study revealed significant water quality improvements, and the Legislature increased funding to $282 million more over twelve years. The Legislature passed a Water Quality Initiative (SF 512) in 2018 that amended the wastewater treatment financial assistance program, created a water quality infrastructure fund, and established a water quality financing program.

1964 League graphic

GIVE THE "GREEN LIGHT" TO GOOD GOVERNMENT FOR IOWA

IV. Good Government Legislation: Making Democracy Work

The Iowa Constitution

The League believes that a state constitution should guarantee protection of people's rights, delineate the framework of state government, and address only major concerns of enduring importance. It should assure separation and balance among the executive, legislative, and judicial branches of government, clarifying lines of authority and responsibility; leave procedural and financial specifics to statutory law; be stated in broad terms to provide for adaptation to changing conditions; be consistent throughout; avoid conflict with the federal constitution or laws; and be free of deadwood, reasonably concise, and easy to understand.

In 1926, the Iowa Constitution was amended to allow women to serve in the Legislature by removing the designation "male." The first female legislator was Carolyn Pendray (1929–35), an educator from Maquoketa. One of her first bills restricted lobbyists to a roped-off area at the back

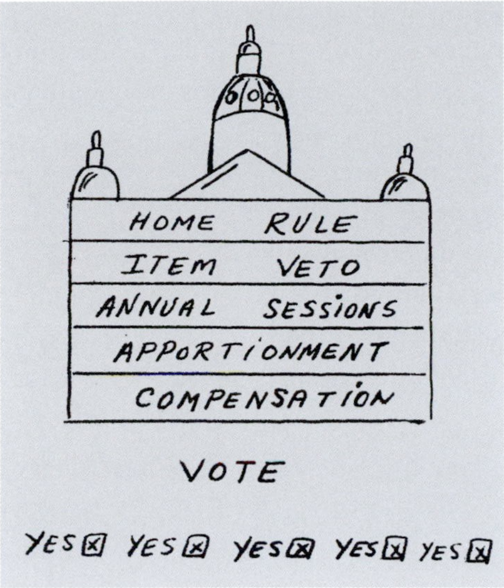

HOME RULE
ITEM VETO
ANNUAL SESSIONS
APPORTIONMENT
COMPENSATION

VOTE

YES ☒ YES ☒ YES ☒ YES ☒ YES ☒

Support for the 1968 constitutional amendment.

of the chamber, preventing them from sitting beside legislators and coaching them on votes— the forerunner of current League-supported restrictions on lobbyists (see Lobbying Appendix).

The League studied and then worked for the passage of the following amendments to the Iowa Constitution:

1962 — Judicial selection based on merit with periodic retention vote by the electorate.

1964 — Constitutional Convention proposals to be submitted to voters for ratification.

1968 — Annual sessions of the Legislature (originally SJR 3 and HJR 9); item veto by the governor for appropriation bills (originally SJR 9); size of the two houses* of the General Assembly and setting their own compensation; home rule powers to cities; and reapportionment provisions (see reapportionment below on the League's work for "one person, one vote" and Reapportionment Appendix). [*During the debates on all the amendments, League members were ever-present, and legislators admired their volunteer efforts. During a discussion about the size of the Legislature, after one senator said he didn't think anyone cared whether the Legislature was made smaller or not, another senator quipped, "Well, the League of Women Voters does!" And, the Legislature adopted the League-recommended number of fifty senators and one hundred representatives, numbers that have remained the same since 1971, the year of implementation of the new size of the General Assembly.]

1970 — Single-member legislative districts.

1970 — Residency requirement included in election laws reform.

1972 — Four-year terms for governor and lieutenant governor, as well as for auditor, secretary of state, treasurer, and attorney general (the latter four offices the League did not support); provision for removal of unfit judges; and repeal of prohibition against lotteries.

1974 — Repeal of allocation of county fines to school districts or libraries; the Legislature given the power to call itself into special session.

1978 — County home rule allowed (originally SJR 3), with implementation beginning in 1981.

1988 — Governor and lieutenant governor elected as a team.

1988 League flyer in support of the 1988 constitutional amendment.

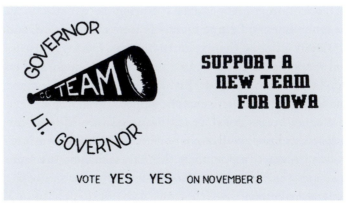

1998 — Rights of Persons: The League spearheaded the successful campaign to add "and women" to the Iowa Constitution, providing not only a statement of principle or core belief but a foundation for legal action by women against sex discrimination, such as lack of pay equity, underrepresentation in elected offices, and sexual harassment or assault.

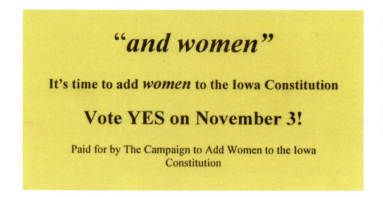

Business card "and women" for League support of the 1998 constitutional amendment (designed by Neysa Picklum of Black Hawk-Bremer League)

The League opposed and worked to defeat the following constitutional amendments:

1963 — Defeat the Shaff Plan for reapportionment that did not meet the League's standards; the League supported a later amendment that passed in 1968.

1992 — Defeat the Tax Payers' Rights Amendment that would have severely restricted spending by cities and counties.

2017 — Defeat a constitutional amendment to require a supermajority of the Iowa Supreme Court in favor of declaring a law unconstitutional.

2018 — Defeat four amendments dealing with the Iowa Supreme Court, term limits for elected officials, General Assembly rules as part of the Constitution, and Marsy's Law/crime victim amendment.

The League supported the following constitutional directives adopted by statute:

1. Civil service system (merit plan) for state employees.
2. Reorganization of the departments of Social Service and Revenue within the executive branch.
3. A unified court system, which refers to unification of the lower court system, bringing all courts under state control, ending the system of municipal- and county-run courts, as well as ending the justice-of-the-peace network; reduction of judicial districts from twenty-one to eighteen, with each court in continuous

session rather than just during specified terms, such as once per week in each county; and the Iowa Supreme Court's adoption of rules of procedure for district courts, with a provision for Legislature rejection.

In other legislative developments related to the Iowa court system, in 2013 the League worked to defeat major changes to the Judicial Nominating Commission and judicial retention. By 2019, SF 638 had made changes to both, which the League opposed. The governor now appoints nine rather than eight members to the Judicial Nominating Commission; each congressional district is to elect one woman and one man rather than rotating between genders; and the chief justice is no longer on the commission. In addition, commission members will select their own chair, and they cannot be reappointed after their six-year terms end. This legislation is being challenged with an upcoming review by the Iowa Supreme Court.

Signature Legislation

Reapportionment (redistricting): Redistricting is the process of re-drawing legislative (voting district) boundaries every ten years following the national census, which is required by both the United States and Iowa constitutions. The purpose is to ensure congressional and state legislatures are representative of the population in order to preserve the "one citizen, one vote" tenet of our democracy.

The Iowa process is lauded as a model for other states because of its nonpartisan method for drawing the districts, with consideration of factors such as population equality, contiguousness, and compactness. The Iowa process limits the participation of elected officials and places the responsibility for configuring the districts with an independent redistricting entity, the Legislative Services Agency. Only six other states (Alaska, Arizona, California, Idaho, Montana, and Washington) have a similar approach to counter gerrymandering, or incumbent manipulation of district formation (see Gerrymandering in Glossary Appendix).

The League's long history with reapportionment dates to 1955, when members began a study of the issue because the Iowa Legislature had not been reapportioned since 1886! The study confirmed public opinion at the time that a receding rural population was over-represented in the Legislature because of a growing urban population. Candace Lambie of Grinnell said of her lobbying days at the Capitol: "I spoke before the Iowa Legislature as League president (1955–57), and we found that the legislators did not know the word reapportionment, so it was our duty to inform them. We sent out five thousand flyers to various people and organizations explaining reapportionment. After some time, a lot of talks, and a lot of paperwork, it was recognized that it was a good idea."

The League formed its resulting consensus of supporting "more equitable representation" in 1956. At the LWVIA Convention in 1959, the League approved "action to obtain fair representation in the Iowa Legislature by a constitutional convention or legislative enactment," and the work of Leaguers across the state began. The 1964 U.S. Supreme Court decision in Reynolds v. Sims, known as the "one man, one vote" decision, added urgency to Iowa getting in compliance with federal mandates for redistricting every ten years based on population census data.

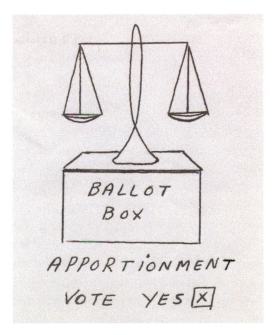

It is worth noting the League's consensus statements below for comparison to the 1968 constitutional amendment and to 1981 procedural provisions, both with similar, if not exact, directives (see Reapportionment in Iowa Appendix).

League consensus on reapportionment (1. in 1966 and 2. added in 1979):

1. Assurance for real and adequate reapportionment every ten years by creating a non-legislative bipartisan reapportionment authority; recourse directly to the Supreme Court with the Court able to make a re-districting plan if the commission fails to do so; apportionment of both House and Senate by

population only, crossing of county lines permitted; and single member districts.
   2. Reapportionment procedures should contain strict anti-gerry-mandering provisions.

Political scientists across the nation have joined the National Conference of State Legislatures (NCSL) in lauding the Iowa reapportionment process. The NCSL reported in April 2018 that "Iowa stands alone in how it handles redistricting responsibilities." That's not only because of the nonpartisan agency producing the every-ten-year plan, but also because of its prohibition of the use of political data, such as the addresses of incumbents, the political affiliations of registered voters, previous election results, and demographic information not required by the U.S. Constitution.

These public statements of support for the Iowa redistricting process are reinforced by the fact that the reapportionment plans created since 1981 have not faced legal challenges. That was not the case with the Iowa Legislature's first plan in 1971 (see Chapter 1).

The League has also worked for equitable school district reapportionment. In the summer of 1981, the League learned that school districts did not have to reapportion their director districts unless they underwent reorganization. The League disagreed with this practice and that fall made the issue a priority, collecting data from 441 school districts to ascertain what methods were used to elect their school board members, along with information about the demographics of the district—data-based decision-making. The League found that several districts had large population deviations between their director districts, and several did not use a method of election provided by the Code of Iowa. These survey results were given to Representative Jean Lloyd-Jones, who requested the attorney general's opinion on several school reapportionment questions. That decision was as follows: School districts must use the latest federal census figures when creating or changing sub-district (director district) boundaries and do so every ten years, with the "one person, one vote" guideline; and school districts must use one of the methods provided in the Iowa Code to elect school board members, and if they use methods b, c, d, or e in Section 275.12 (2), the director districts must be "substantially equal" in population. The Legislature codified this attorney general's opinion in 1983 via SF 485. This outcome for school district reapportionment was the result of the League's data collection and continuous monitoring to ensure compliance with established law, a hallmark of the League method.

Mary Neuhauser, Minnette Doderer, and Jean Lloyd-Jones (left to right) discuss aspects of the 1981 statute establishing the redistricting process.

State Government

As noted above, in 1968, the League worked to pass constitutional amendments that addressed the size of the Legislature and the institution of annual sessions. Other positions taken by LWVIA with respect to state government include opposition to term limits for state representatives and senators and that certain changes in legislative processes could improve the system and the end products.

To that end, the League has studied economical administration by governmental units beginning with a League-supported 1923 bill that called for the consolidation of various entities dealing with agriculture (except for the state fair) into a single Department of Agriculture with an appointed secretary of agriculture. In the next decade, the League supported the 1937–38 establishment of an Iowa State Planning Board. This state agency studied the physical, social, and economic resources of the state and made recommendations to the Legislature regarding their best use and preservation. The board thus provided information legislators needed for better decision-making.

As times changed and the complexity of government increased, this planning board was replaced in 1966 with the Iowa Office for Planning and Programming (OPP), established by executive order, along with sixteen area-wide, regionally oriented planning districts established in 1968—all incorporated into Chapter 473 of the Code of Iowa. Included was Chapter 28E (Joint Exercise of Governmental Power), which made it possible for cities and counties to enter into contracts for services with each other, a League-supported concept to decrease duplication of services and streamline government functioning.

Related to the OPP was the League-supported establishment in

1982 of an Iowa Advisory Commission on Intergovernmental Relations (ACIR). The panel was to create "blueprints" for intergovernmental relations, a concept the League had studied and lobbied for since 1971! The ACIR's goals were to increase flexibility and decrease duplication.

In 1955, the Iowa General Assembly created the Legislative Research Bureau, an entity charged with providing legal and administrative services to the Iowa Legislature on an objective, nonpartisan basis. In 1969, the General Assembly changed the agency's title to the Legislative Service Bureau (LSB) and gave the bureau additional responsibilities. The LSB provided bill and amendment drafting, research, committee staffing, and legal publication services to Iowa legislators. The bureau's professionally trained staff members were precluded by statute from making policy recommendations. A twenty-four-member Legislative Council established bureau policies and oversaw the bureau director's management of the LSB. (1)

In 2003, the Iowa Legislature created the Legislative Services Agency (LSA) by consolidating into a single entity the functions of several existing legislative support bureaus, including the LSB, the Legislative Fiscal Bureau, and the Legislative Computer Support Bureau. The LSA continues to be nonpartisan and to operate under the direction and control of the Legislative Council. Like the LSB, its mission is to provide staff services to all members of the General Assembly. The divisions of the LSA and their respective duties include the Legal Services Division, which publishes official Iowa law documents and provides bill and amendment drafting, legal and legislative research, and committee staffing services. The Fiscal Services Di-

Part of a League pamphlet educating the public on the benefits of a legislative council or other agency to help legislators do a better job.

vision offers fiscal and budget analysis and state government oversight evaluation, and staffs all standing, statutory, Legislative Council, and interim study committees. The Computer Services Division operates the legislative computer systems, providing technology training and support for all legislators and staff and maintaining all hardware and software for the legislative computer network. And the Administrative Services Division distributes print and electronic copies of LSA work products, provides public information services to legislators, staff, and citizens, and offers personnel and finance services to the LSA. (2)

In 1967, the League helped defeat a resolution that would have petitioned Congress to hold a constitutional convention to consider factors other than population in determining the basis of representation in state legislatures, which would open the gates for gerrymandering.

Chapters 21 and 22 of the Iowa Code, the open meetings and records or "sunshine laws," ensure Iowa government at all levels is as transparent and accountable to the public as possible. The law, passed in 1978, states the basis and rationale of government decisions must be easily accessible by the public and any ambiguity should be settled in favor of openness.

For forty years, those following public meetings have seen this law in action. Governmental bodies are required to give adequate notice of time, date, and place of a meeting, and post a tentative agenda to be followed by meeting attendees unless there is an emergency item that cannot be deferred for twenty-four hours. Minutes of meetings must be kept and made available to the public in a reasonable amount of time. Attendees can use cameras and recording devices as long as their use is not disruptive. In regard to public records, all are open for inspection unless the case for closure is specified in law, such as adoption records and certain juvenile records closed to the public.

The open meetings and public records legislation was updated in 2011 to repair gaps in the original laws, including how meetings are reconvened. Legislation that year mandated that all lobbyists must file reports electronically, which also provided better transparency.

In 1983, HF 628 incorporated all county finance measures into one comprehensive law and established uniform accounting and reporting procedures. New legislation directed the Legislative Council to establish a year-round, full-time General Assembly public information officer.

The Government Ethics and Lobbying Bill, passed in 1992, was based on recommendations from the Neu-McCormick Commission, which at the time was the most restrictive ethics legislation in the nation. Specific restrictions in that bill are included in the Lobbying Appendix, but one that all state legislators know: He or she cannot serve as a lobbyist until two years after being a member of the General Assembly.

In 2007, House and Senate subcommittees responded to a long-standing League request when they agreed to announce subcommittee meetings one day in advance, a move that brings more openness to government by providing the public greater opportunity to attend meetings. Attendees also could request to make statements and provide written information.

League "successes" for 2010 included a bill for state government reorganization, which included electronic records availability and public document modernization to improve public accessibility. The bill also directed the Department of Human Resources to reorganize to focus on "community advocacy."

Campaign Finance Reform: Votes Not for Sale

According to a March 2018 Pew Research Center report, 77 percent of Americans support limits on the amount of money individuals and groups can spend on political campaigns. Sixty-five percent of that sample also expressed confidence in the power of legislation to reduce the role of money in politics (view report at www.pewresearch.org/fact-tank/2018/08/30/where-the-public-stands). Such data supports a long-held national League position: Campaign finance regulation should enhance political equality for all citizens, ensure transparency, protect representative democracy from distortion by big money, and combat corruption and undue influence in government. To that end, the League in Iowa has been contributing to the discussion of campaign finance reform in our state since the early 1970s. (All Iowa campaign finance laws can be viewed at ethics.iowa.gov.)

In 1975, HF 431 established the Campaign Finance Disclosure Commission. In the 1980s, the League worked for passage of SF 457, which prevented weakening finance disclosure requirements, added "purpose of expenditures" to disclosures, and clarified the definition of "political commit."

LWVIA President (1989–91) Joan Hartsock addressed a March 1991 press conference about the League's continuing concern for open and honest elections and for maximum citizen participation in the political process that helped ensure the passage of SF 505. That legislation required candidates who did not abide by spending limits to obtain individually notarized signatures on their nomination petitions equal to 10 percent of the votes cast in the last election for that office, a time-consuming task. The law excused candidates who did abide by the limits from this obligation, requiring only that they obtain the legally mandated number of signatures. The law also required public notification of whether candidates abided by spending limits.

The League again worked with legislators and the Campaign Finance

Disclosure Commission in 1999 to improve the Iowa Campaign Finance Law. And in 2001, LWVIA lobbyist Judie Hoffman urged the legislators not to cut funding for the Ethics and Campaign Disclosure Board: "This is a government watchdog agency that couldn't do an adequate job with such draconian cuts. The damage done would outweigh any resulting gains."

In 2001, as a member of the Iowa Alliance for Campaign Finance Reform, the League proposed ten reforms that would make detailed information about campaign contributions available to the public in a timely fashion before an election. All ten proposals eventually were incorporated into Iowa law. And a 2007 bill, drafted after several years of League work, provided for mandatory electronic filing of campaign finance disclosure statements by statewide and legislative candidates. It went into effect in 2010 for new candidates and in 2012 for legislators in office in 2007. Such filings let the public see in advance of an election how much money candidates raised, from whom, and how it was spent.

Another positive campaign finance bill passed in 2008, requiring people with political action committees, or PACs, to reveal their supporters and spending. The legislation targeted groups made possible by a loophole in the federal Internal Revenue Code, Section 527. The Legislature passed more League-supported regulations in 2010: all independent expenditures were allowed only with candidates' knowledge; foreign nationals were prohibited from making independent expenditures to advocate for or against a candidate; and all independent expenditures, with a $1,000 threshold, must be reported within forty-eight hours.

Despite laudable statutory restraints on campaign financing made in the last thirty years in Iowa, issues remain, primarily in the area of out-of-state funders. According to a report released January 16, 2013, by the Iowa Public Interest Research Group (Iowa PIRG), 96 percent of 2012 campaign donations for Iowa's congressional races came from out-of-state funders, including super PACs and other non-party entities. Thirty-seven percent of the outside spending in those races came from groups that do not disclose their funders, causing a lack of transparency in outside spending. As Kramer McLuckie, field associate for Iowa PIRG, pointed out, "When shadowy, out-of-state donors control the campaign coffers, it warps the relationship between representatives and their constituents." And according to 2015 LWVUS President Elizabeth MacNamara, speaking at the LWVIA Convention, "Super PACs raised and spent more than $600 million in 2014 to elect or defeat candidates [nationally], and will continue to raise and spend unlimited amounts because they are supposedly 'independent' from the candidates when, in reality, there are many ways to coordinate [support]." (3)

The League has always stood for sound fiscal responsibility in government, which is reflected in a 1923 League-supported bill called the "Tuck Law." It mandated that county boards of supervisors could not spend more money than they had available—budgeting common sense! That bill also directed that bonds could not be issued without approval by a vote of the county's citizens.

Equity has also been a mainstay of League positions. Thus, the League supported two pieces of legislation on that topic in the 1930s: a 1935 measure requiring the use of a merit system in the selection of public employees and a 1937 municipal civil service bill.

The League's study of state government began in the early 1960s, revealing great overlap, duplication of services, and inflexibility in local governments. In addition, the state legislated most of the important matters of concern to cities and counties due to a nineteenth-century Iowa Supreme Court decision known as "Dillon's Rule." Under the rule, cities and counties had no power not specifically granted to them by the Legislature.

From that state government study and previous work on home rule begun in 1951, the League developed a position in support of city and county home rule and greater local flexibility and intergovernmental cooperation to minimize duplication of services. The omnibus Home Rule Act of 1972—four pounds and 228 pages—contained city and county home rule. The people of Iowa ratified it by way of a constitutional amendment in 1973. But because of a court challenge, it was not implemented until 1975, after the Iowa Supreme Court ruled it was constitutional.

League promotion of the council-manager form of government for municipalities.

THIS GAL'S DATED

Your city government is in the same shape.

Let's bring it up-to-date!

Over 500 cities have switched to the Council-Manager plan in the last ten years. At this rate, it will be the most prevalent form of city government by 1960.

Why?

Before the work for home rule, the League had been involved for years in promoting the council-manager form of government for municipalities. These efforts resulted in legislation that in 1954 became Chapter 363C of the Iowa Code.

In 1976, HF 1076 provided for the adoption of optional forms of county government. And in 1988, HF 278 allowed counties to establish charter commissions to recommend one of several alternative forms of county government to voters for their approval. It was said to be one of the most progressive pieces of local government legislation passed since the early 1970s.

Legislation passed in 1991 allowed for the consolidation of local governments, including mergers between cities, between counties, and between cities and counties. The bill also allowed for different ways to provide local services, which would reduce duplication. That same year, a bill supported by the League in collaboration with other groups changed Iowa law so that bond issues for public buildings could be approved by a simple majority of greater than 50 percent, rather than the previous 60 percent supermajority.

In 2019, SF 634 required cities and counties to have extra public hearings and certify levies with a supermajority vote if the combined total of those levies increased by more than 2 percent. And in 2013, the League fought a push in the Legislature to repeal "Smart Planning Principles" in urban planning.

In 2017, the Iowa League adopted a position on tax increment financing (TIF), seeing it as a positive tool for cities and counties to address economic development, urban renewal, and housing. TIF is a method of financing a project that freezes the tax base (property values) in a designated area. All taxing authorities (counties, cities, schools) continue to receive property tax revenue at the rate when the TIF district (designated area) was formed. As the improvements are made and property valuations and taxes increase, the taxing authority that created the TIF collects all the increased revenues to finance improvements in the TIF area. The authorizing entity continues to collect the increased revenues until the TIF project sunsets and property taxes are reapportioned among all taxing authorities.

But, as usual, after an intense and data-based study, producing reports frequently sought by others for guidance, the League developed the following recommendations (position statements) to improve communication, transparency, and cost impact related to TIF:

1. The Code of Iowa relating to TIF must be amended to include a category specific to alternate energy construction.

2. References to slum/blight should be revised to reflect twenty-first-century terminology.
3. All TIF projects, including urban renewal projects, should sunset within 20 years, even 20 years is detrimental to school funding. The League suggests modifying the law to require local authorizing entities a maximum of 50 percent of the school district tax increment for the duration of the project.
4. Language that allows a 20-year duration for economic development within a TIF district should be amended to require that TIF districts decertify upon project completion. The League further believes that any entity wishing to use TIF in the same area following a project completion must complete a new certification process in its entirety to proceed with a proposal.
5. Structuring TIF debt is important, and the Code of Iowa must be amended to include TIF debt in the calculation against the constitutional debt limit and must include language related to annual payment, as well as interest incurred against the debt.
6. State law for establishing a TIF district must be amended to require detailed communication, including specific plans and outcomes, identifying costs and an estimated return on the TIF investment, and estimating the impact on other taxing entities, to occur among all affected parties before the required three public hearings.
7. Each TIF plan must identify an oversight procedure requiring the local authorizing entity to annually evaluate the effectiveness of TIF use, including costs, at the local level. The League further believes members of the affected communities must be included in the evaluation process to ensure transparency.

Fiscal Policy: Iowa Tax System

LWVIA supports an equitable and flexible system of taxation based on continual study of taxation since 1971. A tax should be evaluated primarily on equity, taxpayers' ability to pay, and adequate yield. A tax should be evaluated secondarily on the size of the tax base, ease of payment and collection, ease of understanding for the taxpayer, flexibility, and a balance between stability and elasticity.

Beginning in the 1930s with a concern for the burden of property taxes, the League has provided citizen input via sharing of data, as well as testimony on various budgets being considered by the Legislature. Some taxation bills to support education, criminal justice, the environment, mental health, and welfare have previously been mentioned in this chapter and will not be repeated here.

Taxation is not only a highly contested topic in every Iowa General

Assembly session, but a complicated and multifaceted issue requiring expertise and space to fully explain. Readers are directed to tax.iowa. gov/iowa-tax-publications for information on current levels of Iowa taxes: individual income, corporate income, sales and use (exemption for food and prescriptions), cigarette, tobacco products, and fuel.

Justice: Sentencing and Corrections

LWVIA supports a justice system that is fair and protects public safety. LWVIA believes that mandatory sentencing has had an adverse impact on Iowa's justice and corrections systems. This adverse impact could be reduced by providing greater flexibility for judges, the Iowa Department of Corrections (DOC), and the Iowa Board of Parole to consider unique circumstances in criminal cases while still adhering to sentencing standards set out in the Iowa Code. The sentencing standards consider such factors as the number of prior offenses, age of the offender, and severity of the crime. (See Justice Appendix for League-created documents on justice lobbying priorities, capital punishment, and felon voting rights. Note that juvenile justice is contained in the Children and Families portion of this chapter.)

Adults: 1978 witnessed the establishment of the Prisoner Employment Program, legislation written primarily by Representative "Beje" Walker Clark. Though the League's Criminal and Juvenile Justice Committee worked diligently and produced data-based documents provided for government decision-making, along with League testimonies at legislative committees, actual legislation passed from the 1980s through the 1990s as a result of their efforts has been difficult to identity.

But in the last seventeen years, the League's impact has been evident. Legislation passed in 2003 reduced mandatory minimum sentences from 85 percent to 70 percent for certain offenders sentenced under Iowa Code 902.12 for less violent offenses. In 2016, sentencing reforms allowed some nonviolent drug offenders to become eligible for parole earlier and created a new, less punitive class of robbery for nonviolent offenses. The next year, the League was successful in its support of narrowing the gap between crack and powder cocaine sentencing, a disparity that leads to a disproportionate minority incarceration rate. The law helped cut that disparity from 1:10 to 2:5—not the ratio the League lobbied for, but an improvement.

In 2018, the League defeated HF 2114, which would have made public the immigration status of a person charged with a crime. During the 2019 legislative session, the League successfully lobbied for passage of needed criminal justice reforms contained in SF 589. The reforms included reducing some Class B felony sentences; allowing judges to oppose mandatory minimum sentences*; expunging records for misdemeanor offenders if the crime was older than eight years and if the individual had not offended during that time period (impacting five thousand Iowans each year); making all public intoxication and consumption violations simple misdemeanors (saving the state $3.6 million in prosecution costs per year); and increasing the threshold value for felony property crimes (which hadn't been updated in decades). In addition, SF 608 gave the offender re-entry program a $50,000 increase, to a total of $390,000. [*It should be noted that the Iowa League's Criminal and Juvenile Justice Committee worked with delegates from the League of Women Voters of New York to pass a resolution at the national convention in 2012. When a state has studied and taken a position on an issue, the state position can be adopted at the convention without going through the study process. New York delegates had contacted Iowa delegates to adopt the New York position regarding sentencing, "The LWVUS believes alternatives to imprisonment should be explored and utilized, taking into consideration the circumstances and nature of the crime. The LWVUS opposes mandatory minimum sentences for drug offenses." The passage of this position is not only an example of a committee's hard work having impact outside of Iowa, but an illustration that national League policy can be altered by state League input.]

Iowa delegates Karen Person (left) and Jo Ann Finkenbinder (right) celebrate the adoption of no mandatory minimums as a national position with New York delegate Jane Colvin (center).

Felon rights: The League, along with the ACLU and other organizations, has long fought for the automatic restoration of voting rights for convicted felons upon release from incarceration. Such became a reality by Executive Order Seven, signed August 5, 2020, by Governor

Kim Reynolds. All felons who have completed their sentences and are on parole or on probation will automatically have a right to vote. Her order excludes those who have committed homicide, manslaughter, or attempted murder, as well as those serving lifetime sentences for sexual crimes or other offenses. This executive order allows an estimated forty thousand Iowans to now exercise the right to vote, along with those who will have felony convictions in the future.

Death penalty: In 1998, 2017, 2018, and 2019, the League, along with collaborators such as the ACLU, helped defeat bills that would have reinstated the death penalty in Iowa. The frequency of attempted legislation on this issue indicates the need for continual vigilance on the League's part and ongoing education regarding the following statistics, upon which the League's position is based:

1. Murder rates in states without the death penalty consistently are lower than in states with the death penalty.
2. Eighty-eight percent of U.S. criminologists in 2009 stated a belief that the death penalty was not a deterrent to murder.
3. Wrongful convictions are estimated in one in every twenty-five cases, or 4.1 percent, twice the number exonerated and set free from death row.
4. The cost of providing the heightened level of due process (legal costs) for those on death row is more expensive than life in prison without parole.

Consumer Protections

League-supported legislation prohibited car title loans in 2007. And in 2017, the League supported legislation that changed asset forfeiture laws, banning seizure of assets valued at less than $15,000, and increasing the standard of evidence to "clear and convincing."

Also in 2017, in response to the Equifax data breach that put Iowans' personal data in jeopardy, the Legislature passed a major consumer protection bill supported by the League. Consumer credit companies no longer could charge for freezes and changes in freeze status, and they must report those changes to other consumer credit companies.

During the 2018 General Assembly, the League successfully defeated the Iowa Small Dollar Installment Loan Act (HF 2485), which would have given "flexible credit lenders" protections. Also defeated was HF 2064, which would have allowed these lenders to add money transfer service fees and receive income tax credits. And in 2019, a League-supported bill banning fees for consumer credit freezes (SF 2177) passed.

1947 produced legislation that guaranteed the right of employees to join unions but also a bill that outlawed labor boycotts and sympathy strikes. Both became Chapter 736A of the 1950 Iowa Code.

Legislation passed in 1984, a Jean Lloyd-Jones initiative, revitalized the rail corridor now operating as the Iowa Interstate Railroad. The railroad mainline is roughly a straight line between Council Bluffs and Chicago and is headquartered in Cedar Rapids.

In 1994, Iowa codified the federal Driver's Privacy Protection Act into Section 321.11 of the Iowa Code. The Iowa Department of Transportation regulates access to motor vehicle records via a request form with rationale.

Related to driver's licenses, the League supported a 2017 resolution by the Iowa General Assembly opposing a federal mandate to take away drug offenders' driver's licenses. Such an action not only would negatively impact mobility, employability, and rehabilitation of drug offenders, but also constitute a loss to the state of federal highway funds. The result: Iowa was allowed discretion over this federal policy without loss of federal highway funds.

In 2010, the League worked to defeat Mid-American Energy's proposal to collect money from ratepayers for a nuclear power plant feasibility study. In 2012, a similar bill was introduced whereby Mid-American sought to shift the cost of building a nuclear power plant to ratepayers, not its shareholders, before a three-year feasibility study was completed. The utility wanted to collect the additional dollars before deciding to build and keep the money even if it decided not to build. The League opposed this bill and worked hard to defeat it.

V. Human Rights Legislation: The Moral Test of Government

"The moral test of government is how [it] treats those who are in
 the dawn of life, the children; in the twilight of life, the elderly; and in
 the shadows of life, the sick, the needy, and the handicapped."
—former Vice President Hubert Humphrey, November 1, 1977.

Depending on the type of legislation involved, the League of Women Voters uses positions originating at either the national or state level as the foundation for working with decision-makers in state government. For human rights legislation, the Iowa League repeatedly has used the League of Women Voters of the United States Equality of Opportunity position, which advocates equality of opportunity in education, employment, and housing for all people, regardless of their race, color, gender, religion, national origin, age, sexual orientation, or disability.

Domestic Abuse

A 1993 law broadened the definition of those covered under the domestic abuse statute to include unmarried couples with children and people who had lived together in the past year. In 1997, a warning was added to the back of marriage licenses per Iowa Code 595.3A. It noted that assault, sexual abuse, and willful injury of spouses or other family members are violations of the law, and family members are provided the full protection of the laws of the state in regard to violence and abuse. An earlier entry in the Children and Families section cites the establishment by statute in 2000 of a Domestic Abuse Death Review Team, funded under Iowa Code 135.108-135.112.

In 2002, legislation again broadened the definition of individuals covered under domestic abuse statutes to include "intimate partners" such as dating couples—a League-supported addition to Iowa's abuse laws. Another law passed that same year allowed a person seeking relief from domestic abuse to use the address of a shelter or other agency as a mailing address for purposes of filing a petition or obtaining utility services.

Discrimination: Equal Rights for All Regardless of Sex

One of the very first legislative priorities for the League of Women Voters of Iowa was the 1926 striking of the word "male" in Article III of the Iowa Constitution, which defined who could serve in the Iowa Legislature. The change opened the way for Carolyn Pendray's election to the Iowa House in 1929 (see Biographies Appendix). Mrs. Pendray worked for property rights for women*, particularly regarding debt collection. At the time, a male debtor could keep specific items from confiscation to pay his debts (a library, clothes, two cows, two calves, fifty sheep, furniture), but a female debtor could not. Mrs. Pendray's bill allowed the same non-confiscated items for women, as well as a sewing machine and $50 worth of poultry. This latter differential was eliminated in Iowa Code fifty years later! [*Despite various published statements, "research does not support this view nor could researchers in the Legislative Service Bureau identify such a connection," according to Suzanne O'Dea Schenken's "Legislators and politicians: Iowa's women lawmakers" (1992, Page 217). *Retrospective Theses and Dissertations*. 10152. https://lib.dr.iastate.edu/rtd/10152.]

The League used its positions not just to pass favorable bills but also to defeat inequitable ones. For example, in 1933 the League helped defeat a bill that would have discriminated against women in public employment. A bill defeated in 1935 had the same aim, but different wording: discrimination against women in tax-paid positions. And in 1937, the League worked to defeat a bill discriminating against women's employment on the basis of kinship and marital status.

In the League's quest to validate the existence of women and their value and integrity, it began study in 1938 of the remaining legal and administrative discriminations that would prevent women from having equality with men. And, twenty-seven years later, in 1965, it became unlawful to discriminate on the basis of race, creed, color, sex, religion, or national origin in housing, employment, credit, education, and public accommodations. In 1972, discrimination based on age and physical or mental disability was added. Part of the civil rights legislation created a commission for reporting and investigating such discrimination, as well as planning programs to educate the public.

In 1975, Iowa House member June Franklin sponsored a bill that required all sample ballots in the state have one-half the names feminine, a small though visible move in the direction of more equality for women. That same year, Representative Minnette Doderer shepherded a bill to remove gender-biased practices in prisons. In county jails, women were allowed to leave during the day to clean their houses and take care of family needs, but men were not. Also, only men were sentenced to hard labor, and a man could not be appointed warden of the Women's Reformatory, both examples of reverse sex discrimination. The bill made all three situations the same for women and for men.

Also in 1975, new legislation prohibited auto insurers from refusing a policy renewal because of the applicant's sex. In 1976, any wording in the Iowa Code affecting the legal status of women was removed or amended.

The League-supported Iowa Equal Rights Amendment (ERA) passed both the 1978 and 1979 General Assemblies but required ratification in the 1980 general election. It did not pass that year and failed again in 1992, despite the work of Leaguers Pat Jensen, Shirley Koslowski, and committee members. The federal Equal Rights Amendment was ratified by Virginia in 2020, the thirty-eighth state to do so, but thirty-eight years past the deadline set by Congress. The outcome probably will be determined by the U.S. Supreme Court.

The removal of masculine pronouns from the Iowa Code and other official state documents began in 1982 and continued with the establishment of a Governors' Committee in 1984. Public employees' titles also became gender-neutral, with, for example, fireman changed to firefighter and policeman changed to police officer.

Comparable worth, a term introduced by Representative Doderer and meaning a system for compensation based on skill, effort, working conditions, and responsibility as the requirements for a position, was passed in 1983 and signed by the governor in 1984. Also, $10 million was appropriated to begin eliminating or amending Iowa laws and regulations that discriminated on the basis of sex. The effort was evaluated by a seven-member oversight committee.

The work of female legislators on the House State Government Committee (four of the seven were League members—Minnette Doderer, Johnie Hammond, Jean Lloyd-Jones, and Jane Teaford) resulted in a 1986 bill mandating gender equity on state boards and commissions. More than twenty years later, in 2009, the same mandate applied to local boards and commissions. The latter bill also added minority appointments in proportion to the percentage of minority population in a city or county.

The League was successful in 1997 in defeating efforts to dismantle the Iowa Commission on the Status of Women, established in 1972 and part of Iowa Code 216A.54. In 2000, equity between men and women for insurance coverage for contraceptives was mandated via SF 2126. If an insurance company provided prescription drug coverage for men's Viagra or other erectile dysfunction medication, the company had to cover birth control medication /apparatuses for women. Iowa was the eleventh state to enact such a mandate.

Sexual orientation was added as a protected category in Iowa's Civil Rights Code in 2007 through the joint efforts of the League and the American Civil Liberties Union. In 2018, the League helped defeat the Religious Freedom Restoration Act (SF 2154, HF 2209), which would have allowed businesses to reject clients whose lifestyles don't match the religious beliefs of the business owners. The League that year also successfully defeated HF 2164, known as the bathroom bill, which would have mandated that transgender/nonbinary individuals use public restrooms consistent with their gender at birth. A similar bill was also defeated by the League in 2019.

Gun Rights

For the last twenty-five years, the League has voiced concerns about handguns and their impact on the health and safety of our citizens. The League supports licensing procedures for gun ownership by private citizens that include a waiting period and background checks, personal identity verification, gun safety education, and annual license renewal. The League continues to work to ban "Saturday Night Specials," also known as SNS, Suicide Specials, or Junk guns, which are inexpensive small pocket pistols or revolvers that have dubious reliability and may be potentially hazardous to operate; enforcement of strict penalties for the improper possession of and crimes committed with handguns and assault weapons; and the allocation of resources to better regulate and monitor gun dealers.

To those ends, the League defeated a stand-your-ground gun provision in 2012 and defeated liberalization of Iowa gun laws in 2015. Because of the current composition of the General Assembly, the League has not been able to defeat subsequent laws on stand-your-ground and the open or concealed carrying of firearms. However, the League continues to monitor gun legislation and present data and positions to legislative committees considering new bills.

Housing

Representative June Franklin of Polk County worked to pass civil rights legislation, a League concern since the late 1930s. In 1969, she led the fight to successfully change Iowa's fair housing law by eliminating the requirement that complaints against realtors and landlords be accompanied by a $500 bond. That provision had silenced many victims of discrimination who could not afford to post the bond. Representative Franklin was the first African American in U.S. history to win a leadership position in either party when she was elected assistant minority leader (whip) for Iowa's sixty-fourth General Assembly. She worked in the areas of education and fair hiring practices, focusing on racial discrimination during her six years in the House.

In 1976, it became unlawful for banks and savings and loan associations to reject mortgage loan applications within a specific geographic area because of the location or age of the property. This bill was in response to discrimination against individuals living in neighborhoods of high poverty or with high numbers of minority residents. This practice was known as red-lining because lenders and realtors would draw a red line around neighborhoods on a city map to identify them as high-risk for loans or residency.

Since the 1930s, Leagues across Iowa had studied and worked for adequate housing. That effort came to fruition in 1996, when an affordable housing bill was passed that included $1 million to help communities set up housing trust funds to better deal with housing shortages. Then in 1997, a League-supported housing development bill made the Department of Economic Development responsible for establishing a local housing assistance program to give technical and financial assistance to local governments and organizations that rehabilitate housing. The bill included funding of $1 million per year for five years from real estate transfer tax money.

Human Trafficking

A League of Women Voters of the United States position is the basis for LWVIA's action on human trafficking: "… opposes all forms of domestic and international human trafficking of adults and children, including sex trafficking and labor trafficking. We consider [it] a form of modern day slavery and believe every measure should be taken and every effort should be made through legislation and changes in public policy to prevent human trafficking …"

Human trafficking is a critical issue for Iowa because Interstate 80, a known thoroughfare for such activity, runs across the state. Action in 2006 by Senator Maggie Tinsman of Scott County resulted in passing legislation making human trafficking a felony in Iowa. Then, in 2016, the League lobbied for successful passage of comprehensive legislation that established the Office to Combat Human Trafficking in the Department of Public Safety, which coordinates efforts across state agencies and between and among criminal jurisdictions; extended the statute of limitations for human trafficking; added human trafficking to the definition of child abuse; and required law enforcement to refer young human trafficking victims to the Department of Human Services.

Minimum Wage

The League in 2007 worked for an increase in the minimum wage in Iowa from $4.25 to $7.25, which is the federal level. The data on such increases indicates that it benefits single women over the age of twenty and 52 percent of families who earn a combined income under $40,000.

Signature Legislation

Rape: Representative Minnette Doderer was a staunch advocate for women who had experienced rape. In 1974, Iowa was one of only five states that required a corroborating witness in order to obtain a conviction of rape—the only crime with that requirement. Her bill eliminated the practice. The next year, Representative Doderer oversaw passage of a bill that eliminated language in the criminal code that allowed judges to instruct juries that the charge of rape is "easy to make, difficult to prove, and more difficult to disprove." The language was not only offensive but created a different standard from other crimes.

In 1976, she tackled two more issues related to rape: marital rape and adequate resistance. The latter was quickly eliminated to make it easier to prosecute rapes. The marital rape issue, however, involved thirteen years of debate! Instead of language defining marital rape, legislators initially supported only a definition of sexual abuse within marriage, which required threats of violence or the infliction of physical injury. With persistence and much persuasion, Representative Doderer and colleagues succeeded in passing a bill that defined marital rape as sex against the will of one's spouse, with or without threat of violence, and made it illegal in Iowa. It becomes a felony through the use or threat of force. Thirty-four states had previously made a similar code change. In 1992, the League worked on preventing rape victims' names from being made public without their permission, eventually contained in Iowa Code 915.20A.

VI. Voting Rights Legislation: One Citizen, One Vote

The right of every citizen to vote has been a basic League principle since its origin. The League's founder envisioned the primary role of the organization to be educating women, and others, to be informed voters, a task she thought would take "just a few years!" Brilliant as Carrie Chapman Catt was, she certainly underestimated the continuing need to educate the citizenry on issues and candidates. A related focus for the League has always been to ensure that citizens have access to voting, a challenge that continues today with recent state actions that have the potential to disenfranchise many. These actions include a requirement for voters' signatures to match and the shortening of absentee voting periods.

Work on voting rights by the League began in 1923 with the passage of SF 359, which increased the time from fifteen to twenty days for applying "for absent voter ballots and increasing the time from 10 to 15 days for the auditor to forward the ballot to the absent voter." SF 350, which passed that same year, provided that for precincts using voting machines, absent voters' ballots were not to be deposited in ballot boxes until after polls closed. They then would be registered on the voting machines by two election judges of different political parties. Legislation to better safeguard primary election procedures for regular and absentee voters was passed in 1926.

In 1927 the League helped defeat a bill that would have required a person to vote in the preceding primary in order to vote in the general election. Also in 1927, the Legislature repealed the act establishing separate ballot boxes for women and men and passed a bill that made a voter's registration permanent until the person was no longer a resident. Iowa was the thirty-third state to ratify the District of Columbia Voting Rights Amendment XXIII, which passed both houses of Congress in 1961 and became law that same year. The League was, of course, a vocal supporter of the amendment!

Signature Legislation

The League helped draft the 1971 bill for a thirty-day durational **residency in the state for voting in all elections**. In anticipation of a Supreme Court ruling banning residency requirements over thirty days and to counter the existing county-by-county residency variations in the state, League members approached the appropriate Senate committee the year before and were rebuffed as "pie-in-the-sky dreamers." When they repeated their concern the following year, committee members claimed publicly that the concept had originated with them, and the bill eventually passed! The League members who had been involved just chuckled: "We don't care who gets credit. We just want good government for the people."

Frank Miller cartoon, "The Right to Vote." Permission granted by the *Des Moines Register*.

The Rest of the League's Hard Work to Preserve "One Citizen, One Vote"

During the early 1970s, the League fought against HF 390, which required dependents' voting residence to match that of their parents or guardians. This effectively disenfranchised students and other young adults who lived in a different location from their parents. The League prevailed, and the bill failed!

In 1973, the League supported election law revisions that included mandatory training of election officials; improved absentee voting procedures, including the delivery of ballots to confined individuals; and statewide registration for voting, not just in counties with populations over fifty thousand or in cities of ten thousand or more. The polls in Iowa could stay open until 9 p.m. as a result of League-supported HF 700, which passed in 1975. And independents and members of minority parties could serve as nonpartisan mobile registrars after SF 590 passed in 1986.

The Iowa Legislature passed election day registration in 1990, but the governor vetoed the law. Same-day registration passed again in 2007, and this time the governor signed it, effective in 2008. The League projected that voter turnout would increase despite the additional burden for voters of having to provide proof of residence and photo identification when they appeared at the polls to register and then vote.

In 1994, the Legislature passed the Motor Voter Bill to comply with the federal National Voter Registration Act (NVRA) of 1993, which required states to offer voter registration opportunities at state motor vehicle agencies. The NVRA also mandated that states offer voter registration opportunities by mail-in application and at certain state and local offices, including public assistance and disability agencies. In addition, the NVRA required states to implement procedures to maintain accurate and current voter registration lists. And since 2002, county commissioners of elections have been required to post signs stating "Vote Here" at each driveway entrance to a building where a polling place is located.

The League began studying the restoration of voting rights for individuals with felony convictions in 2003, and it finally happened in August 2020 with the signing of Executive Order Seven. Like the book title, we are persistent! In April 2019, Karen Person, a member of the League's Criminal and Juvenile Justice Committee, testified before the Senate subcommittee on restoration and conveyed the following key points of the League's position:

> Iowa has been one of only three states along with Florida and Kentucky that permanently ban all individuals with a felony conviction from voting unless the governor restores the right to vote. In November 2018, Florida passed a ballot measure for restoration of voting rights for felons, passed by 64.5 percent of voters and restoring the right to vote to 1.4 million people, the biggest expansion of voting since the U.S. Constitution was amended to lower the voting age to eighteen in 1971. Now Iowa is left as only one of two states in the nation that permanently ban all individuals with a felony conviction from voting. More than fifty-two thousand Iowans have completed the terms of their parole but remain unable to vote, though they are living and working in Iowa communities. African Americans are disproportionately impacted by this ban. League is opposed to requirements such as payment of fines and restitution as this would make it even more difficult than it currently is to restore one's right to vote. Such requirements would negatively impact the poor. The League of Women Voters of Iowa supports HJR 14, a constitutional amendment that takes out the ambiguous phrase "infamous crime," which is a positive step toward dignity for thousands of Iowa citizens.

In 2004, the Legislature passed grant-matching for the Help America Vote Act (HAVA)*, as well as some new regulations for the secretary of state:

1. All voting machines purchased must have a paper trail.
2. When a courier picks up a ballot request or a voted ballot, he/she must leave a receipt with the voter and make sure the ballot is returned to the auditor's office within seventy-two hours.
3. Auditors' staff must put postage, at the county's expense, on each ballot so it can be returned by mail.

[*Congress passed the Help America Vote Act (HAVA) in 2002 to make sweeping reform to the nation's voting process. It addressed improvements to voting systems and voter access that were identified following the 2000 election. The act created new mandatory minimum standards for states to follow in several key areas of election administration and provided funding to help states meet these new standards, replace voting systems, and improve election administration. Iowa's grant in 2018 amounted to $4,608,084, with state matching funds of $230,404, for a total of $4,838,488 primarily for cybersecurity initiatives.

HAVA also established the Election Assistance Commission (EAC) to assist states with compliance and distribute HAVA funds to states. The EAC also is charged with creating voting system guidelines and operating the federal government's first voting system certification program. The EAC also is responsible for maintaining the national voter registration form, conducting research, and administering a national clearinghouse on elections that includes shared practices, information for voters, and other resources to improve elections. HAVA required that the states implement the following new programs and procedures: provisional voting, voting information, updated and upgraded voting equipment, statewide voter registration databases, voter identification procedures, and administrative complaint procedures.]

In 2007, a bill passed that allowed seventeen-year-olds and people not affiliated with a party to serve on election boards beginning in the next election. That same year, legislation passed requiring a paper trail for voting machines, with funding beginning in 2008.

2008 was a busy year for voting issues. Legislation passed that limited special elections by cities, counties, and school boards to four days per year, a cost-cutting measure. Beginning in 2009, school board elections would be held in odd-numbered years rather than every year, saving money for school districts. City, county, and legislative races already were held every other year. Terms for school board members increased from three to four years. In 2009, county auditors also could convene a special precinct election board.

2012 found the League successfully defeating a voter ID law. Five years later, the League and collaborating partners, including the Iowa chapter of the ACLU, failed to defeat a similar measure that requires registered voters to present photo identification cards when appearing at the polls (Election Integrity Bill, HSB 93). The final legislation was not what the League wanted, but the League's Justice Committee worked with the Secretary of State's Office on some adjustments before passage that made the law the least onerous voter identification requirement in the nation, a positive influence by the League. The League is currently focused on helping voters acquire identification cards if they do not have a driver's license, as well as joining others in lawsuits to get the law overturned.

In 2013, the League collaborated with multiple groups to take legal action against the secretary of state. The League and its partners believed he was circumventing the legislative process by establishing new emergency rules aimed at purging voting rolls because of alleged voter fraud. He lost the case at the district court level and appealed to the Iowa Supreme Court. Before the court could hear the case, the new secretary of state voluntarily dismissed the appeal and purged the rules of his predecessor.

Electronic online voter registration went live in January 2016 for those with driver's licenses or non-operator IDs. A longtime League priority came to fruition in 2017 with the new requirement for post-election audits. That same year, seventeen-year-olds gained the right to vote in primaries if they would be eighteen by the time of the general election.

The Legislature passed a "fix" in 2019 for something that kept many voters' absentee ballots from being counted the previous fall. HF 692 required all county auditors to subscribe to the U.S. Postal Service barcode tracking system so that envelopes without postmarks could be tracked for date of mailing and thus allow the enclosed ballot to be counted. Previously, only postmarks made the absentee envelope and ballot valid.

Chapter 9

Taking on the City and County …

Study and Action of Local Leagues

"Study without action is futile, but action without study is fatal."
—Mary Ritter Beard (1876–1958), daughter of Indiana Quakers,
American historian and archivist who played an important role
in the women's suffrage movement, at one time editing the
Suffragist magazine. (1)

Finding Issues for Study and Action

Local Leagues identify important issues in a variety of ways. Newspapers and other media outlets provide information about what's going on in a community, but going to the source of local legislative and regulatory actions can garner more and perhaps better information. Periodic meetings with local leaders can reveal issues or needs the League may want to study and act upon. Examples include the Ames Happening events where public officials report to the community about the past year's results and upcoming plans and proposals, and the thirty-year-old annual State of the City/County presentations in Cedar Rapids and Marion (Linn County League).

The League Observer Corps was a historic avenue for identifying issues and needs. The corps was made up of League members who regularly attended meetings of city councils and county boards and reported back to the membership on topics discussed and decisions made. Local government officials at first found such attendance disquieting or even threatening. League members heard comments such as, "They want 'agendas,' fellas, so you better be prepared," from elected officials unaccustomed to citizen oversight. Some Leagues reported they were labeled "snoops," "spies," and even Bolsheviks. The Pella League observers reported being called "the Leaky Women Voters." Some Muscatine officials branded Leaguers as Communists, while a longtime Board of Supervisors member labeled them the "Plague of Women Voters," even when his own daughter joined the League and her husband became that League's president!

Because of the wealth of information obtained by observers, the practice continued until the advent of televised (now livestreamed) meetings. Former Linn County Leaguer Jean Glaza, like many other corps members, took her preschool daughters with her to observe meetings in the 1960s, as shared in a memoir: "[My daughter] took her little notepad and would take 'notes' just like Mommy, so they have many memories of the League."

Study Defined

One of the principles of the League at all levels—national, state, and local—is to identify issues or problems for study (see Chapter 5 under "variety of resources" and "data-based"). Just what is a study? A group of League members works together to gather relevant information and facts on the topic of interest, being careful to collect data in such a way as to avoid bias. League members use various approaches for such investigations:

- Reading pertinent material from a wide variety of sources;
- Conducting independent research or obtaining data from reliable sources;
- Interviewing people close to the issue; and
- Visiting particular sites (like a school field trip), such as city dumps where most people, other than Leaguers, don't like to tromp around like former Pella Leaguers did, and the Moline, Illinois, John Deere headquarters to view art in a business environment done by Johnson County Leaguers.

When the information-gathering process is complete, the group presents its findings to the League membership in one or more of these formats: a written report, a PowerPoint presentation, a panel discussion, or a graphic representation. League members discuss the findings and come to a consensus, or collective opinion, on their stance as a group. They may decide to pursue one of three courses of action: develop a position statement on the issue to support action to be taken, continue study of the issue for later discussion and consensus, or decline to take a position on the issue.

Sharing Study Findings

"Whenever the people are well informed, they can be trusted
with their own government."—Thomas Jefferson, 1789

Before a League acts on a position it has adopted, members work to educate the public and decision-makers by sharing the information they have gathered. The League is known for the accuracy and clarity of its findings. "What the League has to say has always been intelligent … they've always operated very professionally," Chris Burkett wrote May 8, 1977, in the *Davenport Times*. "They have never personalized arguments or disagreements …"

Leaguers use various approaches for disseminating information:

- Community-wide informational meetings or small coffees with council or board members;
- Written materials such as pamphlets or brochures distributed to libraries and schools;
- Marching in parades, sometimes in costumes related to a current issue and with messages on placards;
- Speakers' Bureau topics presented to community groups;
- Skits and musical performances for an organization or for the entire community;
- Special topic films for viewing at a public event with discussion to follow;
- Presentations on radio or television shows or via podcasts, Facebook, and other internet venues; and
- Position statements, along with supporting data, presented to decision-makers.

Action Defined

Action means working to create change in government policies and practices, including the laws and regulations that impact the citizens of a community, county, state, or nation. And how is that done by Leaguers who are all volunteers and not elected as decision-makers? Well, it is done by 1) being informed on the issue; 2) gathering supporters for the cause by reaching out to individuals and other organizations; 3) understanding the process for legislative or regulatory change so as to approach decision-makers in the most productive manner (see Chapter 7 on advocacy and lobbying); and 4) being persistent in contacts with the decision-makers as well as offering solutions for the issue. "Reform is slow work, and it is for neither the faint hearted nor the impatient," wrote Jon Meacham. (2) More at "League's Process for Doing a Study," www.lwvus.org.

The Things People Will Do to Get Attention

To share study findings, as well as act on an issue for change, an individual or group needs to get the attention of the audience. Marketing research tells us that certain techniques, such as the use of surprise, cognitive dissonance, storytelling, and engaging more than one of our senses, grab and hold people's attention. (3) Public speaking consultant Sims Wyeth encourages speakers or others wanting to get information to an audience to start with the unexpected, make the information relevant, get to the point, and arouse emotion. (4) And, *Forbes* columnist Kare Anderson suggests connecting the content to aspects of the audience members' lives or work, being specific as soon as possible in the presentation, using humor or a pertinent story, and sticking to just three points of information. (5)

Even before marketing research was available and before media advertising bombarded us with the above techniques, members of local Leagues across Iowa used similar methods to share information with their citizen audiences and move decision-makers to action. Here are some of the creative ways that Leaguers got the attention of their audiences.

Black Hawk-Bremer

To highlight the impact of poverty on children and families, the League organized a Welfare Luncheon for the public and invited community leaders. The meal consisted of the food that an Aid to Dependent Children recipient could afford to buy, with statistics and other information on the realities of living in poverty. Though the event was held over thirty-five years ago in the early 1980s, these activities are just as common today as fundraisers for food kitchens and pantries.

Burlington

To increase awareness and provide education about the threat of atomic warfare, the League organized a large public event with bursting bombs and a city blackout, followed by a presentation by the Atomic Energy Commission admiral. It was the 1950s and many citizens thought the possibility of survival and recovery from a nuclear attack warranted individual preparedness, so much instruction by all levels of government was available for adults and children alike.

Grinnell

In the early 1950s, League members concerned about the adequacy of city sanitation counted the number of outhouses in the city and gave the results to the City Council via a map of the outhouse locations, as well as photos of them after rains. The League provided information on the health ramifications of not having sanitation lines to all parts of the city. The City Council "found the money" to install sewer lines in all areas of Grinnell, along with storm sewers—a bonus to the League's work.

Johnson County

To call attention to the poor quality of city water in the 1960s, League members took to the streets of downtown Iowa City and passed out plastic bags containing goldfish swimming in Iowa City drinking water, along with notes indicating that the fish would do just fine in the water rich with micro-organisms harmful to humans. The City Council soon ended its contract with the private water provider and began a city-owned water system with regular testing of water quality.

Marshalltown

Determined to increase voter turnout in the 1950s, League members gave gold feathers to voters after casting ballots. The first time they did so, an election official questioned the practice, but a council member confirmed the League had sought and received permission. People then expected to "be feathered" after voting in all elections, which got rather expensive for the League. So, members decided to give feathers just for school board elections, which had the fewest participants, but also sponsored contests for schoolchildren with prizes for collecting the most feathers from family and friends. Jasper County and Metro Des Moines Leagues also provided feathers as rewards for voting.

So why gold feathers? They may have been easier to obtain than yellow, which was the color associated with the women's suffrage movement dating to 1916. That year at the Democratic National Convention in St. Louis, seven thousand silent women lined the street, elbow to elbow, each with a yellow sash with "Votes for Women" printed on it—yellow for the jonquil flower, the symbol of the suffrage movement. At the end of the line was an immense tableau of kneeling women in black garb extending manacled hands, representing the states where women could not vote. Above them sat women in gray apparel representing the states where women had partial suffrage. Then there were a few women in white, smiling because their states allowed full suffrage. And atop all was a beautiful woman in flowing robes holding the Torch of Liberty. It was quite a dramatic sight and set the stage for future attention-getting approaches employed by local Leagues across the country.

Metro Des Moines

To raise awareness of the need for affordable housing in 1963, the League conducted a bus tour for the public with various stops to see alternative housing and talk with residents. Attendees also learned how different groups developed and paid for each housing venture: a house being rehabilitated by high school students; a city housing project for low-income elderly individuals; and a community center connected to a housing development. This initiative moved decision-makers to envision a variety of ways to increase affordable housing in Des Moines and to find unique ways to finance such endeavors.

Mount Pleasant

In an effort to publicize the benefits of staggered terms for City Council members, a League member wrote a poem based on a familiar Shakespeare line that was placed in the newspaper and on flyers tacked up all over town before the referendum, which was supported by voters:

> "To stagger or not to stagger, that is the question:
> Whether 'twas nobler for the council to suffer the slings and arrows
>   of outraged voters
> Each two years or each four and by petition change them?
> Two years; four years; No more; and so the League would say
> We alternate the terms and thus double the years …"
> —Magdalen Meade (1913–2005), former resident of Mount Pleasant

Oskaloosa

To cut down on the improper disposal of hazardous waste (a 1980s action item for many Iowa Leagues), this League created a window display of hazardous waste materials in a prominent downtown dress shop frequented by community leaders' wives and daughters. The display featured graphic pictures showing the threats hazardous materials posed to children and pets. As a result, the City Council established home hazardous waste drives, installed containers for such waste, and worked with the League on a public information campaign.

Scott County

To dispel fallacies about poverty and welfare, League members in 1968 wrote and presented in various venues in Davenport and surrounding communities a "Welfare Myth" skit. A cast of costumed characters attacked these myths: 1) all poor people are lazy; 2) welfare makes our taxes higher; 3) only the poor are subsidized; 4) all welfare recipients cheat; 5) welfare provides a Cadillac living; and 6) welfare supports all runaway fathers' kids. The script is available in the Davenport library archives for anyone who could still benefit from its message since some myths take a long time to die.

Local Leagues in Action

Here are summaries of some of the study and action projects accomplished across the decades by the eleven current local Leagues, all undertaken in addition to their work on national and state issues (covered in Chapters 5 and 6) and on voter registration activities (examples in Chapter 11). Iowa local Leagues have always tackled problems and gotten things done. Each local League is prefaced with identifying information, which includes the names of LWVIA presidents from that League as well as women from that League who have served in the Iowa Legislature or in another state-level elected capacity. The length of a local League's portion of this chapter does not reflect the entirety of its work, but what was available for review.

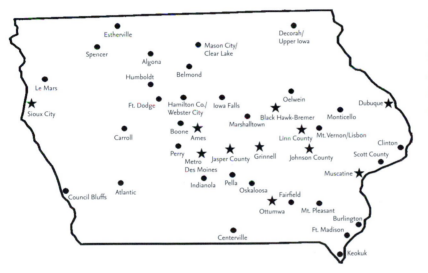

Map of Iowa with current local Leagues starred and former Leagues (Chapter 10) bulleted.

"Don't tell my mom about the bullying going on at the high school! She will get the League involved and there will be a lot of noise about it, with stuff in the paper, and heads rolling!"—overheard from a teenage boy during a garage band practice in 2000.

League of Women Voters of Ames & Story County

LWVIA Presidents: Lois V. Holler 1944–46; Minnie C. Arthur 1949–51; Loya Getz 1959–63; Jackie Manatt 1991–93; Jan Beran 1995–97
Iowa Legislature: Johnie Hammond, House 1983–95 and Senate 1995–2003, as well as a 2005 inductee to the Iowa Women's Hall of Fame; Jane Greimann, House 1999–2005; Lisa Heddens, House 2003–21
1995 League Member of the Year: Jan Beran for her authorship of the LWVIA 75th anniversary publication *A Voice for Citizens, A Voice for Change* and a 1998 inductee to the Iowa Women's Hall of Fame

Ames was an early local League, established in 1925. In cooperation with other organizations in the area, it initially provided Citizenship Schools (see Chapter 5). In the late 1920s and early 1930s, due to national interests and directives from the national League, Ames studied disarmament and efficiency in government. For state concerns, members focused on child welfare and marriage laws.

This League was very busy in 1941 when members studied differences in rents in this college town, finding the average rent to be $38.50! Members looked into prices for various goods in Ames versus other college communities, as well as the status of rooming houses in Ames and the curriculum of maid schools (see Glossary Appendix). They did a housing survey by following postal routes and noting empty houses. And, they began an interest in juvenile delinquency, which became both a local and state study for many years.

1948 found the League researching and then publishing "This is Ames," a citizens' handbook given to each household. Members also began working with other local organizations on annual voter registration drives; in 1952 they registered more than fifteen hundred people in a single day!

In the 1950s, the League studied and acted upon the following: Ames school district reorganization; the hospital facility and that board's plan for expansion; and a land annexation study, the results of which were published in the local paper and thus impacted the final annexation ordinance. And, just to keep all Leaguers busy, they began a multiple-year study of waste management, formerly called garbage, which culminated in 1963 in the construction of a state-of-the-art Resource Recovery Plant.

In 1960, the League published and distributed "Voting Information for Armed Services Personnel." Members then studied physical education facilities in Ames and the school district, which led to the construction of a municipal pool at Ames High School. The League also studied fair housing regulations, and its report led to the adoption of an improved ordinance.

"Save the Depot" is another example of the Ames League's contributions to the community. Leaguers collected and shared colorful stories related to the old railroad depot and designed T-shirts as part of their successful campaign to prevent demolition. The renovated Ames Depot now is the home of a variety of downtown businesses and shops.

Transportation is a perennial issue in college communities, and the League has studied, restudied, and provided recommendations to decision-makers on this matter. Recreation is high on the list of community members' priorities, so Leaguers have studied and made recommendations on needs, programs, and facilities in all of Story County.

For the seventy-fifth anniversary of the League of Women Voters in Iowa (1995), the Ames League prepared a fifth-grade curriculum about Carrie Chapman Catt; held a public children's event at the state Capitol, with Jane Cox presenting a portion of her "Yellow Rose of Suffrage" play; and helped raise funds for Iowa State University's Catt Hall. Jan Beran, Ames Leaguer and LWVIA president at the time, wrote a seventy-fifth anniversary history of the League as part of the commemorations.

And most recently (2014), the Ames League sponsored a public forum on a bond issue for funding of a new convention center and remodeling of ISU's Scheman Building.

Why Don't I Just Quit?

It seems to me that every year I'm busier than before.
I'm tempted to resign from League,
Instead I take on more!
For surely there's a reason.
I'll have more time, I tell myself.
Right after the rush season.
Besides, the League gals are my good friends,
I couldn't let them down.
These surface reasons I advance
The real one's further down.
I think the answer lies somewhere
Deep within myself.
I want to see my talents used,
Not rusted on the shelf.
I want America to be
A better place to live;
Just talking won't improve it,
We also have to give.
I want to find myself among
The workers, not the floaters—
And this is why I am neck-deep
In the League of Women Voters.

—*Ames voter*, September 1975

Black Hawk-Bremer President Cherie Dargan and Geri Perreault with Jane Cox as Carrie Chapman Catt, 2018 League Brunch.

League of Women Voters of Black Hawk-Bremer
— Black Hawk and Bremer counties
(name since 1974; formerly Waterloo League, then renamed
Waterloo-Cedar Falls in 1964)

LWVIA President: Jane Teaford 1979–81
Iowa Legislature: Gertrude Cohen, House 1965–67; Jane Teaford, House 1985–93; Pat Harper, House 1985–93 and 1987–91 and Senate 1997–2003; Joy Corning, Senate 1985–91, lieutenant governor 1991–99 and Iowa Women's Hall of Fame inductee 2004; Deborah Berry, House 2003–17; Doris Kelley, House 2007–11; Timi Brown-Powers, House 2015–21

In 1941, some Waterloo women attended an International Affairs Institute at Grinnell College, co-sponsored by the Grinnell League, and came back so impressed that they organized the fourteenth League in Iowa. One of their earliest activities was a "School for Political Effectiveness," which featured five sessions on impacting the political process. They hosted 150 women from sixty organizations and gave out 2,700 political primers to distribute in the community.

In the 1950s, when only men served on boards and commissions, Leaguers wanted to get a "first woman" board member, particularly on the Board of Education. The easiest way to do that was to secure an appointment when a male member resigned. A group of League members did just that, telling the school board president: "We want a woman appointed. We have a well-qualified person—Georgie Nye—and if you don't appoint her, we have the votes to defeat the appointee who will have to run in the next election." Mrs. Nye was appointed, served ten years, and then was president of the State Board of Education. During this decade, the League worked hard to broaden its membership, with a special effort to add African American members. And in 1969–70, members worked on school desegregation, producing an informational booklet with data on educational gaps between white and minority children.

In the 1970s, the League studied air pollution in Black Hawk County and shared the data with the public and with those industries contributing to the pollution. In the 1980s, the League studied: 1) the county jail, with recommendations for needed structural improvements and services for inmates; 2) the Cedar Falls Recreation Center; and 3) childcare needs in the area. The League used billboards to educate the public about good government and soil conservation. Members also sponsored a well-attended Energy Efficient Home Tour as part of their work on energy conservation.

The 1990s found this League commemorating the seventy-fifth anniversary of the passage of the Nineteenth Amendment and working with various women's organizations in the area to increase awareness of women's issues and citizens' rights through public presentations and media opportunities. During this decade, the League studied early intervention for children at risk, mental health updates/managed care, and hazardous household materials. As part of the hazardous materials study, Leaguers educated and monitored retailers on the display and labeling of such materials, which resulted in a high level of compliance. For such efforts, the League earned a Governor's Volunteer Award. And, in 1992–93, members studied libraries in the area, successfully campaigning for increased funding for renovations in Waterloo, and expanding study and action to libraries in other towns in the county.

League study and action can include panel presentations for the purposes of gathering facts and presenting information as a public educational tool. In 1997, this League held two noteworthy panel discussions: "Our Libraries: Meeting Challenges in a Digital World," with library directors in Cedar Falls, Waterloo, and surrounding locales sharing challenges and opportunities for library services in their communities; and "Affordable Housing in Black Hawk County," which featured a variety of presenters experienced in housing alternatives and funding.

The League sponsored "Local Voices—Citizen Conversations on Civil Liberties and Secure Communities" in 2005. In 2010, for the ninetieth anniversary of the passage of the Nineteenth Amendment, the League recognized Mrs. Jens (Anna) Thuesen, the first woman in Black Hawk County to vote after the passage of the Nineteenth Amendment. Mrs. Thuesen was honored during the Register's Annual Great Bike Ride Across Iowa (RAGBRAI) stop in Waterloo (Leaguers are always "with it" for the changing times as well as for taking advantage of all kinds of opportunities to highlight the work of the League.) At this event, the League also raffled off a flag that had flown over the White House, donated by U.S. Senator Chuck Grassley, and held an open house at the Thuesen farm for the riders and their support crews.

Always concerned for the citizenship education of the young, Leaguers in 2011 sponsored an essay contest for middle schoolers titled "Why is it important to vote?" The League recognized the winners and shared the essays publicly. The contest has become a yearly Partners in Education outreach activity. Also in 2011, to honor local women who had been elected to public office, League members did a "drive around town" to present them with certificates of appreciation. Local news media covered the effort. And, related to the League's local study of water, a community conversation titled "Water: Too Much—Not Enough" consisted of a panel that discussed the relationships between runoff, flooding, and water quality.

First meeting of the Iowa division of the Upper Mississippi River Restoration (UMRR) Committee, including LWVIA Board member Sue Wilson from Dubuque, a supporter of preserving the Mississippi River watershed.

League of Women Voters of Dubuque

LWVIA President: Mary Rae Bragg 2016–19
Iowa Legislature: Pam Jochum, House 1993–2009 and Senate 2009–21

Dubuque organized a League in 1944, during World War II. Members initially pursued the study of war-related topics adopted by the national League: price control, rationing, and conservation of goods in the community. After the war, Leaguers turned their study and action to state of Iowa topics, such as child welfare, the city manager form of government, and public school reform.

Regarding local issues, this League studied the need for a new Central Fire Station by interviewing firefighters and touring the existing facility and by gathering information on fire stations in like-sized communities. Members educated the public and urged support of a bond issue for a new facility, the third such bond issue. Their get-out-the-vote telephone campaign may have been responsible for the passage of that bond issue and construction of a new fire station. They also worked for several years to get the courthouse restored due to "bats in the belfry"—actual bats! Because they were keen on renovation, this League also campaigned successfully for the funding and construction of a new law enforcement center.

Study of the traffic pattern on one of the city's main thoroughfares, Central Avenue, resulted in a successful League proposal to the City Council to widen the street. In 1974, the League studied the issue of landfill relocation from a flood plain to a place that met Iowa standards, as well as long-term alternatives to total dependence on a sanitary landfill, such as recycling and incineration of waste to generate electrical power. In 1996, a public forum addressed the topic of minimizing waste, illustrating how local Leagues may look at the same issue in different ways over the years as needs change.

The League took up the issue of campaign finance reform beginning in the 1970s and rallied the community to sign a congressional petition after a public information campaign involving various media outlets. This issue appears to have a life of its own because in 1997, this League and others in Iowa were continuing to work for improvements in campaign financing, which still is an issue across the United States. From the words of League member Pearl Spencer in 1957 on such persistence:

> "… because we inherit[ed] the zeal of our suffragist forebearers, we are not discouraged if we do not quickly achieve a desired governmental reform. We can afford to take a long look; we can sustain the rigors of a long haul … we can withstand temporary

failures and march right ahead, sowing the seeds of truth and justice ... we know that if the seed has been good, it eventually will sprout, and if we tend the plants carefully, they will grow."

In the 1980s, the League conducted a motor oil collection campaign across Dubuque as well as a bus tour titled "Vanishing Acres—Where Has All the Farmland Gone?" as part of a study of land use and city/county urban development.

And across its seventy-five years, this League has held many public forums, addressing such issues as compliance with Title IX in school physical education, domestic abuse, housing, juvenile violence and juvenile justice, gang and criminal activity, and "The Plus and Minus Methods of Governing." Recently, this League came into the digital age by installing electronic message boards on key travel routes in the city, with varying statements encouraging people to vote in upcoming elections.

Digital boards encouraging Dubuque voters to go to the polls, November 2018.

League of Women Voters of Grinnell — Poweshiek County
(first known as the League at Grinnell College)

LWVIA Presidents: Alice Phelps 1939–41; Anna Louise Strong 1943–44; Louise Ross 1951–53, Candace Lambie 1955–57; Ferne Norris 1957–59; Terese Grant 2019–21
Iowa Legislature: Janet A. Carl, House 1981–87

The *Grinnell Herald* reported April 28, 1923, that a group of Grinnell women had formed a chapter of the League, which "will be open to town ladies and Jr. and Sr. girls," with these activities: "the education of women to an intelligent use of the [voting] franchise, work for welfare legislation regarding maternity and child labor laws, and removing the legal and political disabilities of women [through legislation]." The Grinnell League has been working on those activities for the last almost one hundred years.

One of the founders of the Grinnell League was Laetitia Moon Conard (1871–1946), who came to Grinnell in 1906 when her husband, Henry S., began teaching botany at the college. She earned a Ph.D. in 1899 and later taught economics and sociology there as well, after raising their children. Mrs. Conard had been active in the suffrage movement, ministered to the poor and needy via the Uncle Sam's Club, and was one of the founders of the Iowa Civil Liberties Union. She ran for Iowa governor on the Socialist ticket in 1932; for Congress in 1935; and for U.S. Senate in 1936, the first woman in Iowa to do so. Mrs. Conard stated in a 1933 interview that her welfare work, World War I, and the women's suffrage movement moved her into socialism, though her Quaker upbringing in Pennsylvania was a definite influence. Some would say she was a woman ahead of her time (a true Leaguer) because her positions and causes grew to be mainstream issues in future decades (see Chapter 2 Appendix).

In the 1930s, the League held Citizenship Schools routinely for area residents, both women and men. Thanks to the presence of Grinnell College, the League was able to bring a number of prominent speakers to the community. This included Chester Davis, a Grinnell alumnus and agriculture specialist who was director of the Agriculture Adjustment Administration, one of the most important of President Franklin Roosevelt's New Deal agencies. In 1965, former President Dwight D. Eisenhower was a guest speaker in this small Iowa community! And in 1941, the League co-sponsored an International Affairs Institute at Grinnell College that attracted many and was lauded in newspapers across the state because of its relevance to wartime issues in Europe. In 1949, the national League recognized the Grinnell chapter as an enthusiastic and flourishing local League.

Like many local Leagues, the Grinnell League worked in the 1950s for a change to a council-manager form of city government. In the 1960s, the League helped establish, in collaboration with the Ministerial Association, a Human Rights Commission to deal with fair housing per the 1965 Iowa Civil Rights Law and helped develop a unified recreation program for the city with a recreation director and a commission.

In the 1960s the League also completed a study that established

Skit by Grinnell Leaguers Margaret Gullett, Marilyn Stover, and Carol Nielsen derived from the 1960 Broadway musical "The Fantasticks."

the need for a mental health center in Grinnell, which illustrates what League founder Carrie Chapman Catt said many times: "If the League isn't five to ten years ahead of others in our identification of needs, then we should just disband!" Grinnell, like the Scott County League and others, early on—over fifty years ago—saw the need for improved mental health services, which Leaguers continue to recognize and work toward today.

The 1970s were busy years for this League. Projects include providing solid waste management information to the city and recommending recycling of newspapers and other materials; campaigning for school redistricting needs and new schools, including support for multiple bond issues across several years; working with groups within the county to prepare a land use plan; preventing the City Council from putting a parking lot in Central Park. Yes, Leaguers not only got laws and policies enacted, but they also stopped some legislation. The Grinnell League helped implement the needed reapportionment of city wards to align more fairly with the population.

In the 1980s, the League worked to establish an enrichment program for gifted students and an after-school program. They also supported new construction of schools in Grinnell. In 1981, Grinnell Leaguers compiled information on appointed board and commission members to document any disparities in gender or ethnicity they could work to reduce.

In 1997 and again in 2002, the League compiled options for public transportation in Grinnell and needed services outside the community, sharing them with the public. In addition, the League held public presentations on the State of the City, of the County, and of the Schools

Grinnell Mayor Dan Agnew (*back row center*), at the Council meeting for the 19th Amendment Proclamation, along with Grinnell League members, spring 2020.

periodically in the early 2000s and produced and distributed a "Know Your County" publication (updated in 2014 and made available online and in paper form). Members also undertook an initiative to provide information on food, energy, and housing resources to low-income individuals and families in 2010 and provided statistics on poverty to the public. Over the last fifty-plus years, this League has taken on projects that deal with assisting those in poverty through funding made possible by the Campbell Fund, a trust fund "for relief of the worthy poor in the City of Grinnell."

This League held a public program on judicial reform in 2012 and one on human trafficking in 2015. Members also began advocating in 2012 for a rental housing inspector due to low-income housing concerns. The city took action on that position in 2016.

When the Grinnell Mental Health Center closed, this League in 2014 studied the impact and provided information on accessing mental health services that could be made available in the future. That same year, the League began a celebration of International Women's Day, which has since been held annually. Members also sponsored well-attended public forums in 2016–18 on the following topics: the Constitution, reduce/reuse/recycle, civility, and alternatives to domestic violence.

Members of the LWVIA Criminal Justice Committee, including LWVIA President Bonnie Pitz (left), Jasper County, while visiting with a House leader in regard to mandatory minimum sentencing.

League of Women Voters of Jasper County
(since 1996, but formerly Newton League)

LWVIA Presidents: Gladys Nelson 1937–39 and Bonnie Pitz 2012–16
Iowa Legislature: Gladys Nelson, Iowa House , 1951–57

After the founding of this League by Gladys Nelson in 1934, members worked for the passage of Aid to Dependent Children grants, as did a number of local Iowa Leagues, by writing letters to their representatives and repeatedly visiting the Legislature. The League also supported tuberculosis testing for food handlers.

In the 1940s, this League initiated a proposal for the city manager form of government for Newton while promoting the purchase of voting machines. The latter became a reality five years later when collaborative community efforts yielded sufficient funding. To get support for a gas franchise bond issue, Leaguers called everyone in the phonebook to remind them to vote on the extension of natural gas to Newton, an outdated approach now with Contact Lists on phones and computers, but it worked then and the measure passed. And, this League first started discussing mental health needs in 1948. Members began a formal study in 1960 that culminated in the establishment of a mental health center in 1964, sixteen years after the need was first identified but well ahead of most communities.

In 1957, after the League studied the amount of fluoride in city water and shared the results publicly, the City Council acted upon the League's recommendations.

Beginning in 1961, the League found a novel way to engage high schoolers: a scrapbook contest, with a prize, of course. Students produced scrapbooks that identified state legislation passed in the previous year, along with an assessment of how each would impact citizens.

"The League could not be an 'ambulance-chasing' organization, whose spokespersons were positioned for immediate comment and dramatic pronouncements on each new trauma rocking the nation. Its abiding strength lay precisely in the careful crafting of its positions and the longer perspective born of its sustained attention to questions chosen for agenda action," was a directive from historian Louise M. Young in the 50th-anniversary commemoration of the LWVUS. So, in the 1980s, this League chose to attend to various critical issues in their community. They studied adult day care, with a center eventually opening in nearby Newton. Other topics studied included: domestic violence, which propelled the establishment of services to assist victims; the consolidation of home health care services, which, again, came about as a result of the League presenting its study data to decision-makers; and the need for a new jail. A study of urban renewal and tax increment financing (TIF) found, among other things, that the city compensated owners of property to be demolished for their loss, but not renters who were evicted. A personal appeal to the City Council by Leaguer Mary Manatt about the discriminatory nature of this compensation plan yielded a change in policy, providing renters compensation when they were forced to move due to the demolition of their residences.

Kicking off the League's work in the 1990s, the City Council approved a League-supported proposal to ban open leaf burning. Then the League collected extensive data on low- to moderate-income rental housing availability, which the city of Newton used as a basis for its criteria for rental housing assistance applications. And the League took on a study of county-wide library services and funding due to increasing rural circulation costs and a state property tax freeze. The results of the study helped the library trustees to better understand the issue, and they and the League then encouraged the county Board of Supervisors to raise funding for rural library services, which the board did soon thereafter.

The 1990s and 2000s found this League studying ambulance services and their funding as well as the structure and function of county government, use of parks and recreation, recycling and waste management, public transportation in Newton, and roadside vegetation.

Memories event in spring 2019 honoring nine longtime League members: Nancy Lynch, Rebecca Reiter, Nancy Porter, and Barbara Beaumont (back row) and Carol Spaziani, Pat Jensen, Claudine Harris, and Jean Lloyd-Jones (front row). Sally Stutsman was not available for the photo.

League of Women Voters of Johnson County
(has been known in the past as the League of Women Voters of Iowa City as well as the Johnson County League of Women Voters)

LWVIA Presidents: Mary Martin 1928–30; Grace Stromsten 1930–33; Marie Cherrington 1933–35; Laura DeGowin 1946–48; Jean Lloyd-Jones 1971–74; Pat Jensen 2003–05, as well as a member of the LWVUS Board 1982–86

Iowa Legislature: Minnette Doderer, House 1965–70, Senate 1971–79, and House 1981–2001, as well as a 1979 inductee to the Iowa Women's

Hall of Fame; Jean Lloyd-Jones, House 1979–87 and Senate 1987–95, as well as a 2003 inductee to the Iowa Women's Hall of Fame; Mary C. Neuhauser, House 1987–95 and Senate 1995–99; Sally Stutsman, House 2013–17; Amy Nielsen, House 2017–21

1995 League Member of the Year: Pat Jensen

The first local League in Iowa—still in existence—was founded in 1920 in Iowa City, home to the University of Iowa. A local physician, Zella White Stewart, was in Chicago for a medical conference and happened to attend the first League of Women Voters Convention while there. She decided that Iowa City needed a League organization. A group of women already organizing Citizenship Schools then formed the Johnson County League, and they continued these schools not just in Iowa City but in other communities within the county. They began a long collaboration with the university in 1923 with a free, three-day Citizenship Conference featuring speakers of national prominence in the fields of economics, political science, and history.

Most League activities in the 1920s and 1930s continued to focus on educating women and immigrants about voting and how various levels of government operate. This League accomplished this goal in part through a Speakers' Bureau established in 1923 with presenters on various ballot issues, which continued for many years. Members also campaigned for permanent voter registration in Iowa City, which was accomplished in 1930.

Adoption of the council-manager form of government resulted from League action in 1950 and work that continued to 1966 when the League mobilized to defeat a proposed measure to end it. The League studied the need for a new County Care Facility in the 1950s, resulting in the construction of a new facility with a county supervisor on its board.

"The time is ripe, rotten ripe, for change; then let it come!" said James Russell Lowell (1819–1891), poet, abolitionist, Harvard professor, and ambassador to Spain. Acknowledging that the time was "ripe," this League took action to get written directions for voting posted in voting booths, a state law that had been ignored in Johnson County! In the late 1950s, the League began a campaign for voting machines that included researching their use, petitioning local officials for their purchase, and demonstrating them to voters. Persistence paid off, with voting machines being introduced in Iowa City in 1964.

As part of a university community, this League has always been interested in adequate housing. The League conducted its first survey of housing during World War II. In the 1960s, Leaguer Carol Spaziani worked with the City Council to create a Minimum Standards Housing Code after a tour of rentals found units with no windows. In another study, after obtaining the results from a formal rental housing survey of nearly five hundred landlords, fifty Leaguers each spoke informally to the ten with the most rental properties. The results revealed a discrepancy between the impersonal survey ratings and the personal discussions about whom they were renting to, revealing definite discrimination. The League shared its survey results at a City Council public hearing, which helped push the city to adopt the first Fair Housing Code in Iowa in August 1964. It is noteworthy that this League was the strongest non-religious group to work with churches and religious leaders in Iowa City on this issue (a local NAACP branch did not form until 1979). At the League's instigation, the city adopted a local building code in this time period to replace the general state building code the city had been using. The League performed another housing study in 1990, with a formal position taken and updated in 2003 and 2016; and two Leaguers have served on the Housing and Community Development Commission since the latter date.

As a result of her extensive work on housing, Mrs. Spaziani shared in a March 2018 interview:

> League gave me skills in community organizing, research, report writing, and interaction with community leaders that I had not had before.

Johnson County League members conducted other studies in the 1960s on the following topics: mental health services in the county; support for the first subdivision ordinance; and a childcare study that led to the creation of an older teens study group, summer day camps and after-school care for children, and the first group home for runaways in Iowa. Leaguer Mori Costantino was appointed to the Iowa City Civil Rights Commission and later served on the state-level commission.

Visitors to Iowa City's downtown will see the efforts that began many years ago as the result of the urban renewal study and actions by this League. After educating themselves about the multiple aspects of urban renewal, members provided information to the public to help increase understanding of the concept and its potential results. They urged the Iowa City Council to apply to the U.S. Department of Housing and Urban Development for urban renewal funds to save the tax base of the Central Business District. Listed below are a half-dozen of the League's "21 Principles for Iowa City's Urban Renewal," still applicable today for communities in renewal:

- Efficient public transportation (bus)—an issue in 1969 and still fifty years later;
- Adequate short- and long-term parking;

- Streets in the Central Business District well-designed for circulation and accessibility, as well as elimination of through traffic;
- Fair market prices paid for each parcel taken under condemnation proceedings;
- Provision of land for university expansion adjacent to its teaching core; and
- Compatible uses grouped in districts.

Urban renewal activities also led to the creation of Project Green (Grow to Reach Environmental Excellence Now) , an organization that worked for beautification of Iowa City; a recommendation for a planning/zoning study that yielded a comprehensive plan for the Iowa City metro area; and support for a large annexation vote that passed. Leaguer Flo Beth Ehninger wrote of this busy and productive time for Leaguers in Iowa City:

> I know that I built a circle of true friends because we had a worthwhile goal and pulled together through thick and thin (and varying opinions) to build what I feel is a better world … when one gets involved in meaningful goals along with good people, the endless meetings, dirty dishes in the sink, peanut butter sandwiches, and co-op babysitting all seem worthwhile …

Janet Shipton was an active member of this League's Observer Corps during the late 1960s. Observing city council, county supervisor, and school and other board meetings was a common practice of local Leagues at the time. Mrs. Shipton attended Iowa City Library Board meetings regularly and recommended that the board ask the Johnson County Board of Supervisors to include a line item for the library in their budget since a large number of people living in the county used the Iowa City public library without the county providing any funding. The library board agreed and requested that the county board provide an appropriate level of funding based on county users. The Johnson County Board of Supervisors responded positively to the request and has provided user-based funding annually to the Iowa City Public Library ever since. League observation and recommendation to decision-makers worked in this situation as it has for other Leagues across the state.

The League studied the Home Rule Charter concept for Iowa City and reached a consensus in 1973. That decade saw this League studying comprehensive planning for all governments in Johnson County and coordination of these plans among jurisdictions and school districts. The 1990s found this League studying county government, offering several recommendations for streamlining services, which officials implemented. One such result was the Joint Emergency System that unified emergency communications between the Johnson County Sheriff's Office and the Iowa City Police Department. The League also hosted international visitors interested in grassroots democracy and the electoral system and presented "public living room" discussions focused on ideas such as affirmative action, and advertising and the media in political campaigns.

In the early 2000s, LWVUS was advocating for computerization of voting across the nation, asking all state Leagues to petition their states to do so. Johnson County's Barbara Beaumont was adamant that a paper trail was needed to back up computerized voting. She and other Johnson County League members were Iowa delegates to the national convention and lobbied for LWVUS to add a paper trail to its position on computerization of voting. The assembly of delegates supported their recommendation. The LWVUS amended its position, and thus its promotional materials, to reflect the need for a backup paper trail for all computerized voting. How important those paper trails have been to many election results across the nation in the past almost twenty years!

This League undertook a massive study of regional development, involving meetings of the Johnson County Council of Governments over many years. The initial study began in 2001, with a position established in 2002 and updated in 2006. (Some League positions may require updates periodically as issues and situations change.) And as a novel way to impact the interest of future voters in government in 2014, this League worked with the area Girl Scout Council to create a unit on good government that when completed, earned a girl a badge. In 2016, League members developed Living in a Caucus State training for the public about Iowa's first-in-the-nation caucus.

Most recently, "Making Connections" has been incorporated into this League's yearly program of events. These are social gatherings with wine and light refreshments held in a member's home, where League members and guests can learn about and discuss topics related to League positions. Informed individuals on a topic present to the attendees, followed by a question-and-answer session. Examples of topics include "Tracking Progress in Engagement and Implementation in the Cedar River Watershed 2008–18," "What Drives Fake News?" and "Human Trafficking: Definition, Prevalence, and Advocacy."

League of Women Voters of Linn County
(began as the Cedar Rapids League; then in 1965 became the Cedar
Rapids-Marion League; now Linn County, with a
separate Mount Vernon Unit)

LWVIA Presidents: Abbi Swanson 1993–95; Audrey Hauter 2007–09; Myrna Loehrlein 2009–12
1995 League Member of the Year: Abbi Swanson

This League initially formed in 1920. During its early years, the League organized and conducted Citizenship Schools. This was the modus operandi for many local Leagues because of the national League's promotion of education for new female voters and anyone else desiring such information. This League had a series of "ups and downs" during its formative years, and little information exists on its activities until the 1950s. The League's study and action topics were: a major streets study; a bond issue for new high schools; twenty-five thousand copies of a "Handbook on Cedar Rapids" designed, printed, and distributed door-to-door (revised in 1961–63); city planning; local education programs; successful action on the council-manager form of government; and a two-year county survey. Former active Leaguer Jean Glaza reminisced about those years:

> I remember going to Mrs. Farmer's home many mornings to study and work on our League topics. We always had playpens (the predecessor of the Pack 'n Play), diaper bags, bottles, rattles, etc., packed in with our League papers, but somehow we managed to learn a lot and find time to present our materials to others at our meetings. Sometimes our work sessions were almost like the day care centers of today!

The 1960s found this League active in these areas: urban renewal; preparation and dissemination of a county handbook on government; poll reporting for national television; needs at the county home; vocational education; air pollution control; and a Citizens Committee for Public Housing for the Elderly, which failed in a funding referendum initially but came to fruition in later years.

In 1986, in a joint venture with the then-independent Mount Vernon League, the League helped secure the passage of a local option sales tax, in no small measure thanks to the fifty thousand "Twenty Questions on Local Option Sales Tax" brochures designed and distributed by League members.

The 1990s found this League involved in a Charter Commission to change the form of city government, as well as a Community Restorative Justice Task Force. During this same period, the League instituted and continued yearly State of the City and State of the County luncheons*—one each for Cedar Rapids, Marion, and Linn County. Mayors of the two cities and the Board of Supervisors chairperson are the presenters at these annual meetings, and attendance is always high. The LWVLC uses the events as fundraisers for its public education initiatives. The League also re-established legislative forums after a lapse of several years. [*Two former LWVIA presidents, Audrey Hauter 2007–09 and Myrna Loehrlein 2009–12, both of Cedar Rapids, have been involved from the beginning of these "State of" events, and they have something else in common. After moving to the area, both were invited by a Leaguer to League events. When their personal situations made joining the League possible, they were given small jobs at first (like bringing doughnuts to a candidate forum) as they learned about the organization at all three levels and met lots of informed and interesting people.]

Marion Mayor Nick AbouAssaly addressing the sold-out crowd of 600 at the 2020 State of the City event at the Cedar Rapids Marriott sponsored by the League of Women Voters of Linn County. The event is held annually, as is one for the City of Cedar Rapids.

In 1998, this League headed an effort to change the government in Cedar Rapids by forming a study commission to provide public information on the types of city government allowed in Iowa. Despite considerable opposition to the formation of this commission, the League obtained the required number of petition signatures, and the commission provided a considerable amount of educational material to interested citizens. Their hard work exemplified Thomas Jefferson's advice, "Democracy is cumbersome, slow, and inefficient, but in due time, the voice of the people will be heard and their latent wisdom prevail."

In the early part of the twenty-first century, this local League again led the campaign to inform voters on options for forms of city government, as well as published and distributed a "Directory of Elected Officials."

More recently, the League conducted a public education initiative on water quality, starting with a Water Fun Day at a local park where water-based activities for families included creek water testing, illustrations of flooding in a watershed, and demonstrations of the use of permeable pavement options. Then the League sponsored a formal water quality forum with representatives from agriculture and water conservation, along with a chemist and a news reporter.

In 2018, this League restored a League in nearby Mount Vernon by organizing it into a unit of the Linn County League. Individuals in various parts of Iowa have expressed interest in forming new Leagues, and Myrna Loehrlein of this League has offered her expertise to assist in the process. And Linn County Leaguers participated in Expungement Clinics, where they learned how to assist released felons in completing the forms needed to apply for restoration of voting rights.

League of Women Voters of Metro Des Moines — Polk County

LWVIA Presidents: Flora Dunlap 1919–20; Grace Brown 1920–21; Florence Prather Pierce 1921–22; Nellie G. Tomlinson 1922–23; Carrie Louise Daniels 1923–24; Ann Drake 1924–25; Julia B. Mayer 1925; Adelyn Hunt 1935–37; Louise Moon 1975–79; Joan Hartsock 1989–91; Mary Daily Lange 1997–99; Marla Sheffler 2005–07; Dr. Deborah Turner 2015–16, who served on the LWVUS Board 2016–2020 and was elected president June 2020, and is a 2013 inductee to the Iowa Women's Hall of Fame

Iowa Legislature: Jo Ann Zimmerman, House 1983–87, lieutenant governor 1987–91, and 2005 inductee to the Iowa Women's Hall of Fame; Janet Petersen, House 2001–13 and Senate 2013–2021; and Marti Anderson, House 2013–19

Lieutenant Governor: Sally Pederson, 1999–2007, and 2004 inductee to the Iowa Women's Hall of Fame

This League, home of historic suffrage leaders and activities as well as central to the development of the state League, is our much-advantaged local League. Its proximity to the Statehouse provides easy access to legislators, government agencies, and lobbyists, and as part of the largest metropolitan area in the state, it has an enviable base of prospective members! In fact, for many years, the state League was fortunate enough to have a staffed office in Des Moines.

The Des Moines League was formed in 1920. The fledgling state League held its first convention in this central location in September of that year, almost one year after the organization of the Iowa State League on October 2, 1919. Much of the work done by this young League was the result of national priorities: women in industry, child welfare, independent citizenship for women with specific attention to property rights, compulsory education, and "social hygiene." Social hygiene was a late nineteenth- and early twentieth-century movement to protect and improve the family as a social unit through control of venereal disease, regulation of prostitution and vice, and dissemination of "sexual education," which later became a field of study alongside that of social work and public health.

This League had the honor of hosting the 1923 National League of Women Voters Convention with these eminent speakers:

- Herbert Hoover, a native Iowan, who would become the thirty-first president of the United States in 1929;
- Sir Robert Cecil of London, a British lawyer and the architect of the United Nations (see Biographies Appendix); and
- The Honorable Florence Allen, first female judge on the Ohio Supreme Court, or any state supreme court for that matter, and one of the first two women to serve as a federal judge (see Biographies Appendix).

THE NATIONAL LEAGUE OF WOMEN VOTERS IS NOW IN SESSION IN DES MOINES

"Ding" Darling cartoon from 1923 honoring the National League of Women Voters Convention held in Des Moines. Permission granted by the University of Iowa Photo Archives and the "Ding" Darling Wildlife Society.

The early Des Moines League also organized Citizenship Schools in the 1930s that included such topics as "The Role of Money," "Agriculture, Business, and Industry," "The Expanding Role of Government," and "Unemployment Insurance." These were not the basic "voter participation" topics espoused by the national League, nor were they presented by League members themselves, but by professionals, many with partisan identities. During this decade, this League also accepted partisan payment of some League expenses, which was and is counter to League principles. As a result, the national League sanctioned the Des Moines League in 1943, and the chapter disbanded.

The Des Moines League re-emerged in 1944 after the national League president visited to discuss the meaning and practice of nonpartisanship. In 1947, the League published and distributed fifty thousand copies of a citizens' handbook titled "You are Democracy." In 1948, members studied the council-manager form of government, helped achieve its passage by just 880 votes, and received a Lane Bryant Award for their tenacious efforts. They also produced a "Guide to Government in Polk County" for distribution to schools and adult education classes. The League updated and republished the guide in 1963, 1965, and 1967, and Des Moines public schools used it as a textbook for many years.

The League conducted a city-wide survey of minority employment in certain jobs at the request of the Mayor's Commission on Human Rights. League members interviewed 1,100 individuals and found that 92 percent favored employment based solely on ability and not race. And, Leaguer Louise Noun chaired a home rule study, which the *Iowa League of Municipalities Magazine* published in 1952. In 1957, the Carrie Chapman Catt Memorial Fund awarded this League the Freedom Agenda Award for initiating and teaching adult education classes using the seven Freedom Agenda booklets on American heritage, freedoms, and rights and responsibilities of citizens. And in 1959, this League faced down a challenge to the council-manager form of government. The referendum to continue with this arrangement won by 11,452 votes—an example of Leaguers staying in for the long haul!

Studies conducted in the 1950s included fair employment practices, the handling of juvenile offenders in detention homes and police departments, and recreation needs and facilities.

And then came the "rocking '60s!" The League created and presented to various civic groups a slide show (before videos and PowerPoints) titled "What about our 14,000 Sub-Standard Homes?". The *Des Moines Register*, called by many around the state THE Iowa paper, reported about the Des Moines League:

Outside of government agencies, no other organization has been more instrumental in keeping the issue of low-rent housing alive since 1961 when the Des Moines voters defeated a low-rent housing proposal.

The League continued to campaign for low-income housing, and the Des Moines Jaycee-ettes presented Leaguer Edna Brody with a Woman of the Year award for her volunteer efforts in that arena. In 1968, the League supported the city's request to use Section 23 of the Federal Housing Act to provide housing for low-income families—persistence pays off!

Collaboration with other organizations grew in the 1970s when the Des Moines League was one of six organizations represented on the Section 208 Waste Water Study's Citizen Advisory Committee. During this decade, a growing number of League members were appointed to city and county boards and commissions. More than 200 people from businesses, government, and the public attended a Metropolitan Government Conference at Drake University. The Jaycee-ettes presented another Woman of the Year award to Leaguer Nadean Hamilton. Metro Des Moines, the new name for this League, participated in ABC's election night reporting, which provided national exposure for this Heartland League. The League facilitated a meeting on the social, economic, and racial concerns of the inner city for the Des Moines Housing Council, an outgrowth of the League's Housing Task Force. The League received a state League Action Award for this initiative and its work on housing issues. In addition, in their spare time, this League successfully advocated for a new Polk County Jail.

In the 1980s, Des Moines Leaguers monitored the Polk County Land Preservation and Use Committee during its inventory of land-use changes since 1952. This League also distributed twenty-five thousand "I-Save" energy audit pamphlets to elementary schools in Des Moines and the surrounding area. And, Leaguers conducted a study of governmental services in the metro area in collaboration with the Chamber of Commerce of Polk County, the Des Moines Tax Association, and the AFL-CIO; it was published and distributed to area libraries.

Mary Daily Lange of Des Moines was LWVIA president from 1997 to 1999, and her vast experience with restorative justice not only guided her local League but the state League's Juvenile Justice Committee. She emphasized the grit it takes to get things done, sharing her own family history—her maternal grandmother marched for suffrage in Kentucky, and she and Mrs. Lange's mother "were not afraid to state their opinions and always worked to make needed changes in their communities."

In 2001, the League organized a public event titled "People, Politics, and Money," with speaker Rick Kozin of the Iowa Alliance for Campaign Finance Reform. And in 2002–03, LWVDM led the Youth Vote Coalition Project, one of just twelve cities in the nation chosen that year to do so. Youth Vote provides a nonpartisan guide for implementation in a community, with the aim of increasing political awareness and civic participation of youth.

More recently, the Des Moines League studied domestic violence, and members presented a domestic violence simulation titled "A Walk in Her Shoes." League members also facilitated teenagers' participation in the teen dating violence and abuse prevention curriculum "Love Doesn't Have to Hurt: Perspectives on Domestic Violence," and organized community discussion groups featuring the book *Black and Blue*.

The League organized a public education event in 2012 on the Iowa Merit Selection System for Appointing Judges, which fosters fair and impartial courts for our state. Then-Chief Justice Mark Cady gave the presentation.

This local League participated in a 2015 *Des Moines Register* promotion called "Give a Damn Des Moines! Vote!" The series of events aimed at young professionals encouraged them to register to vote, participate in caucuses, and go to the polls. The venue for the events was a popular "watering hole" downtown, the Des Moines Social Club, with bands, art, videos, and food trucks. That same year, longtime League member Jean Basinger received the ACLU of Iowa Louise Noun Award for her leadership of Iowa Women Prisoners and Citizens United for the Rehabilitation of Errants, as well as her involvement in other restorative justice initiatives and organizations. And, to be in the mainstream of public interest in 2017, the Des Moines League sponsored a well-attended public event featuring a journalism professor discussing "fake news."

Leaguers greet and register attendees at a Give a Damn Des Moines! Vote! event titled "It's NOT a Damn Debate!" The event featured Republican and Democratic party chairs answering moderator questions. Pictured are Kathy Kahoun, Judy Dirks, Karla Brizzi, Barb Adams, Phyllis Franklin Devine, and Karen Person.

1995 League Member of the Year: Sue Johannsen

Dorothy Ann "Nan" Waterman arrived in Muscatine after the League's formation in 1964. She rose to prominence in the League, becoming LWVIA president in 1969–71 and then LWVUS vice president twice and secretary once in the 1970s, the second Iowan to serve on the national League board. Mrs. Waterman went on to become the second chairperson of Common Cause, based in Washington, D.C., where she continued to lobby Congress and the executive branch on good government issues common to both the League and Common Cause.

Local Leagues have always had a lot of creative members and leaders working for improved government. Muscatine was fortunate to have some musically talented women, particularly in the 1960s, and here is just one of their creations!

Sung to the tune of "Love and Marriage"—1955 Frank Sinatra hit from Thornton Wilder's "Our Town" production:

Town and city—Town and city
Their affairs concern a League committee that is like no other.
For towns are run and things are done
all differently from one another
Schools and taxes—Schools and taxes
There are many people wielding axes
What to do with town dough?
Where there's doubt
The League finds out and then goes out to let the town know
There are certain local issues that can cause confusion
But the League gets all the facts and then dispels illusion
Forestation? Recreation?
How does zoning help with the population?
Did we need new school sites? A bigger gym?
What's just a whim and what's a good foresight?

Foresight is evident in the many local studies accomplished across the years, as detailed below.

1967: Urged the support of Title I Migrant School, a summer school educational and day care program for the children of migrant workers in the area, accomplished with federal funding.

1967–68: Supported a new fire station when insurance ratings caused higher premiums due to inadequate facilities and helped get the bond issue passed.

1968: Studied and recommended diversified recreation programs for all ages with a full-time recreation director and a recreation commission, which came to pass through collaboration across the community.

1969: Urged support of the new high school bond issue, which passed.

1972–2000 studies included county government; city annexation with consideration to land use, i.e. planning and zoning; elected and appointed city boards and commissions with the League advocating successfully for seven years staggered terms for aldermen, for which this League was awarded the Lee Kirkwood Memorial Action Award from LWVIA in 1982; day care facilities, with the League producing and providing to the community annually a brochure of such facilities; long-range planning for Muscatine County, particularly land use along the Highway 61 bypass; role of the Board of Education; local option taxes with an emphasis on who benefits and how; low-rent housing issues; city-county law enforcement, which resulted in a joint communications system and consideration of other city-county consolidations; city-county ambulance services, which resulted, after many years of collaboration with stakeholders, in Emergency Medical Services being handled by the Muscatine Fire Department; solid waste management, after which the city began the Kleen Sweep Recycling program; human growth and development curriculum for the school district with implementation based on League recommendations; space needs for county government and the courts; and the impact of hazardous farm chemicals on the area's aquifer.

Occasionally a League will host a community event when it has not studied an issue but members see the need for a public forum where both sides of the issue can be presented. Such was the case for this League in 1996, when members organized a Riverboat Gambling Forum for their community on the banks of the Mississippi River.

Along with data from their own findings, local Leagues provide information to the public on a variety of topics related to the positions of the "parent organizations"—the national and state Leagues. The Muscatine League has been very active in this regard, providing an example of the role local Leagues across Iowa play in disseminating information to the voting public:

1988–89: Sponsored the U.S. 88: A New Road to the White House forums, using nonpartisan materials from the Roosevelt Center for American Policy Studies.

1994: Held a Juvenile Justice Forum with a panel made up of Muscatine's senator and representative in the Iowa Legislature, an associate county attorney, the chief of police, and a Department of Juvenile Court Services representative organized by Muscatine's first male League president, Police Officer Rob Yant.

2008: Sponsored Iowans Talk Back on Peace and Security, a topic from the Talk Back on Foreign Policy Issues, a United Nations Association initiative for congressional districts.

2009: Organized a meeting at which local utility personnel shared information on renewable energy sources and air quality, as well as an update by county officials on area flooding and government response.

2010: In cooperation with Muscatine's state representative, the League organized a community forum on air quality, with a panel of professionals discussing the health issues stemming from poor air quality.

2013: Organized a second forum on air quality with a representative from the Department of Natural Resources discussing the three designations for meeting air quality standards.

2015: In collaboration with the 50–50 in 2020 organization, helped organize a presentation on gender equity on local boards and commissions, a goal based on a 2009 Iowa law.

2018: Organized a presentation by representatives of the local utility company on energy generation from coal, solar, and wind.

Community Reads have become a good avenue for engaging the community through the reading and discussion of books that explore current issues such as diversity, climate change, and civility in government. The Muscatine League, in collaboration with the local community college, selects books available at the public library, advertises them to the public, and organizes gatherings for presentations and discussions about the books. The League has coordinated the following Community Reads: *Voting Rights and the Constitution: Past and Present* and *Buying the Vote: A History of Campaign Finance Reform*, both led by University of Iowa College of Law professor Todd Pettys; *The New Jim Crow*, led by Adrien Wing of the University of Iowa College of Law; *Lost Buxton*, led by author Rachelle Chase, exploring a fully integrated community in southeast Iowa that thrived in the early 1900s (see Glossary Appendix); and *Reading with Patrick*, with author Michelle Kuo speaking about literacy needs in our communities.

Dr. Adrien Wing, University of Iowa College of Law, and Muscatine Community College President Naomi DeWinter answer audience questions at *The New Jim Crow* Community Read.

The Muscatine League has encouraged League members to hold public office, and several have, including county board members Joni Axel (2008 inductee to Iowa Women's Hall of Fame) and Sandy Huston; County Auditor Leslie Soule; and City Council members Gayle Sayles and Sue Koehrsen (the latter now of the Ames & Story County League). And Leaguer Sarah Lande was the Iowa Sister States organization executive director, establishing a relationship between Iowa and northern China's Hebei Province in 1983. In 1985 and 2012, she planned visits to Muscatine by Xi Jinping, long before and soon after his appointment as president of China. Mrs. Lande wrote *Old Friends: The Xi Jinping-Iowa Story*, for which the Chinese People's Association for Friendship with Foreign Countries recognized her in 2013 as an honorary friendship ambassador.

League of Women Voters of Ottumwa — Wapello County

LWVIA President: Dr. Gail Quinn 1999–2001
Iowa Legislature: Mary Gaskill, House 2003–19

Wapello County may have formed a League in 1920, right after the formation of the state League, though records only substantiate a 1969 founding. At that time, Leaguers began studies of: city government, with the council-manager form eventually adopted; the city water department; and hazardous waste in their community. Many local Leagues studied hazardous materials in the 1960s because of a growing concern about land use, which involved soil and water quality.

The League's first action campaign was in support of the city's annexation of farmland for an industrial park. After a study of the issue, League members, along with the Ottumwa Labor Council and the Ottumwa Advisory Committee, worked for approval of the proposal. It passed by just 187 votes!

The League also studied the Ottumwa School District's facilities and took action, again with other organizations in the community, to pass a bond issue. It did not succeed, but the League and others persisted, and in subsequent years the public did support funding upgrades of various school buildings.

1983–85 found this League studying disaster emergency preparedness for the city and county. This study revealed two major problems: 1) a serious lack of understanding of the Multi-Hazard Disaster Plan by the people responsible for carrying it out; and 2) the lack of an effective emergency warning system for all parts of the city and county. The League then worked on solutions, which included the immediate education and coordination of responsible responders and a new siren system, which was finally installed in 1989.

The *Ottumwa Courier* featured this League in a January 30, 1989, opinion page article titled "Women Voters Don't Just <u>Talk</u> Issues, They <u>Study</u> Them." The article was based on an interview with Leaguer Darlene Peta, who stated, "League studies broaden your knowledge of an issue, and all sides of that issue … when we decide to act, we are persistent."

2013–14 saw a series of "Community Conversations" on the state's redesigned legislation for mental health services. In 2017, the League organized a series of well-attended public events on gun safety. And 2019 found this League collaborating with other organizations in the community for a Voting Rights Vigil and a Women's Equity Day. The former was aimed at bringing attention and support to reinstatement of the 1965 Voting Rights Act and supporting passage of the federal voting rights legislation. The latter event involved the mayor's proclamation marking the hard-won battle for women's suffrage and family events focused on the importance of voting.

"Fire alarm" group of Leaguers at the State Capitol lobbying for HJR 14 felon rights bill February 2020

League of Women Voters of Sioux City — Woodbury County
(formerly the Woodbury County League)

Long before President Franklin Roosevelt's 1930s comment, "The real safeguard of democracy ... is education," League founder Carrie Chapman Catt was preparing to educate women to be informed voters through Citizenship Schools. The Sioux City League organized these schools in the community for several years after its founding in 1920. The League performed a number of additional community service activities before it disbanded in 1943 to concentrate on community needs resulting from World War II. A new League reorganized after the war in 1949.

The League undertook study and action on the council-manager form of government in 1954. For three decades, the League continued to monitor this form of government in Sioux City, successfully campaigning in 1988 to preserve it. For this, the League won the state League's Lee Kirkwood Memorial Action Award. The League also researched and monitored flood control of Perry Creek for years until the city completed the recommended actions in the first decade of the twenty-first century. As a Leaguer mentioned previously, "We are persistent!"

In 1990–91, this League was "wasted," helping to implement Siouxland Recycles, a program for recycling waste such as magazines, plastic bags, and bottles. An estate donation allowed the League and other local organizations to rent a semi-trailer for city-wide waste collection once a month. Leaguers and sometimes their children staffed the trailer for the widely publicized recycling program. Eventually, in 1995, the city took over responsibility for recycling collection, which continues today in a much-expanded form.

The LWVSC campaigned to remove juveniles from the county jail and successfully lobbied for the creation of the Sioux City Juvenile Detention Center. In 2000, this League hosted a public forum with student panelists lobbying for the creation of a skate park, a goal they achieved when the City Council created Cook Skate Park (perhaps those students will be future League members). The Sioux City League worked for a one-cent local option sales tax to support public schools and for the expansion of Highway 20 to four lanes—both accomplished. The League is proud to partner with the Sioux City Mayor's Youth Commission to involve youth in the political process. The two organizations co-sponsor school board candidate forums and work together on town hall forums with local state legislators, including students in the planning process and at the events.

Recently the League designed, organized, and led a "Caucus 101" event where members explained the purpose and procedures of an

Iowa caucus. Perhaps it is on YouTube for other Iowa local Leagues to use! Other local issues studied by this geographically "way-out-there" League include childcare services and funding, health care and mental health services, and school district programming.

League of Women Voters of Sioux City board members and replica suffrage wagon, February 2020.

The February 2020 Sioux City Legislative Town Hall with State Representatives Chris Hall and Tim Kacena and State Senator Jackie Smith. The League Moderator is Korey Cantrell.

The youngest delegate to the 2019 LWVIA Convention in Ames, Aman Alahi, Sioux City, with Ames host Karen Kellogg.

Chapter 10

"Where, Oh Where, Have All the Flowers Gone?"

... Former Local Leagues

SINCE THE STATE League's founding, women across Iowa have organized a total of forty-five local Leagues. Early data on the number of total members is scant, but in 1975 twenty-eight Leagues posted a statewide membership of 2,304. Today we have eleven local Leagues made up of eight hundred members (nearly 20 percent men), with at least two new Leagues forming.

We know that in its first fifty years, the League got laws passed and worked hard to "get government down where you can reach it" (Iowa League President Loya Getz, 1959–63), through informing the public about issues and possible solutions, registering people to vote, and lobbying the Legislature for laws to improve the lives of Iowans. So why did membership decline?

Times changed. Women's dominion over civil society and their exclusive hold over the home changed as they joined the workforce. For centuries, women, particularly those who had the time to participate in civic activity, used their education and skills to form collective organizations for the improvement of American society. They advocated for the poor in settlement houses for immigrants and the homeless; supported the arts; led children's activities at churches and in organizations like the Girl and Boy Scouts; became involved in politics; raised funds for schools and hospitals; and participated in numerous other activities in their communities. Such volunteer work began during the birth of our nation. During the Revolutionary War, women raised money, provided needed supplies and amenities to soldiers, and supported the independence movement. It continued through the Civil War when women volunteered as field nurses and assisted with the acquisition of clothing and food for soldiers.

As more women entered the workforce, spurred by the need for labor during World War II and accelerating into the 1970s, the amount of time a working woman had for volunteering in her community greatly decreased. Add to that the increase in the divorce rate beginning in the 1970s, which resulted in many one-parent, woman-headed families and added to the time burdens of many women with children. Also, during the last fifty years, nonprofit organizations such as United Way, the Salvation Army, and the Red Cross have increased the services they offer and now do a lot of the work formerly done by volunteers. Women's volunteer associations are not the only groups to witness a decline in membership. Many organizations, from fraternal societies to mainline churches to bowling leagues, have seen a similar drop.

Despite fewer members of the League today than in the past, we still are "an organization of doers," as reported in 1956 by a Mount Pleasant newspaper: "... they dig in at the local level ... if a town requires proper playgrounds, the League [takes it on] ... if there is a slackness in garbage disposal, Leaguers figure out why and suggest a solution. They are not afraid of the hard questions or the hard work to get to a resolution ..." And as we move into the future, we need to keep in mind that today's pool of potential volunteers may have higher expectations for a volunteer experience, perhaps desiring to make a visible contribution; and that technology is our friend not just for communication, but for holding meetings and discussions, fundraising, and social networking.

The following Leagues have disbanded, but they made significant contributions to their communities when they existed. A lack of activities noted below for these former Leagues does not mean they accomplished nothing, but rather that records of their achievements have not been preserved.

This listing begins with the League of Colored Women Voters of Des Moines, founded in August 1919, two months before the organizational meeting of the Iowa League. Across Iowa and the nation after universal women's suffrage became enshrined in the Constitution, well-educated and industrious women worked for the betterment of their communities and state through involvement in Leagues or other organizations that held the same guiding principles: to educate voters about the responsibilities of citizenship and to inform on issues facing local, state, and national decision-makers.

One such talented and energetic organizer was Sue M. Wilson Brown, who founded the League of Colored Women Voters in Des Moines (see Biographies Appendix), as reported by the *Iowa State Bystander*, the oldest black newspaper west of the Mississippi and the voice of the Iowa African American community. The *Bystander* printed announcements of the League of Colored Women Voters' meetings beginning in August 1919, in advance of the formalization of the Iowa League of Women Voters on October 2, 1919, which occurred simultaneously with the dissolution of the Iowa Equal Suffrage Association. Mrs. Brown was the first president of this newly formed League, with a board of seven who met monthly at the Community Center at Ninth and Mulberry in Des Moines.

Mrs. Brown attended the last Iowa Equal Suffrage Association convention in Boone, speaking on the "Political Education of Colored Women." The speech was about the Citizenship Schools the Des Moines group planned to present to women in the community. Early in March 1920, Iowa League President Flora Dunlap, a resident of Des Moines, attended a meeting of the League of Colored Women Voters. She shared information from the February 14, 1920, Chicago convention where attendees had formalized the organization of the League of Women Voters of the United States. Dunlap urged the Des Moines "women to prepare themselves for the big task now confronting them," the job of helping women to become informed voters. Mrs. Brown and three other members of the Des Moines League of Colored Women Voters went as delegates to the first convention of the new Iowa League held in Des Moines that September.

Members of the League of Colored Women Voters volunteered in various capacities at the polls for a fall 1920 Des Moines election, and many also belonged to women's clubs in Des Moines. In May 1921, the *Bystander* published an address by Mrs. Laurence C. Jones, president of the Mississippi Federation of Women's Clubs, who was on a speaking tour of the Midwest. In her address titled "Party Politics as Affected by Woman's Suffrage," much of Mrs. Jones's message for the future, when women could vote and belong to political parties and other organizations working for change, read like League of Women Voters' positions:

Sue M. Brown, State Historical Society of Iowa, Des Moines.

1. More emphasis on the social condition, including the elimination of child labor, more equitable school laws, improved conditions in hospitals, more libraries and playgrounds, and improved juvenile justice.
2. More stringent protections for the safety of food and drink.

3. Improved housing, particularly for the poor.
4. Increased wages for girls and women who work in offices and factories.

Mrs. Jones also forecast that participation in parties would increase, parties would broaden their platforms to include the above-named issues, and more men and women would seek public office. (1)

The *Bystander* reported that the Des Moines League of Colored Women Voters worked for the passage of a "streetcar franchise" at a special election in fall 1921. After that victory, members may have turned their interest to arms limitation. Mrs. Brown shared an address by President Warren Harding on that topic at a meeting that fall, and arms limitation was part of the program handed down by the National League of Women Voters for local League study. This League certainly would have been aware of that program given its communication with Iowa League of Women Voters officers such as Flora Dunlap.

So, what happened to this League after 1921? The *Bystander* was not published from 1922 to 1926 due to financial difficulties, and the organization was not mentioned in articles published in 1927 and beyond. A search of other archival materials provided no further information. What is apparent is that there was a group of highly educated and community-minded African American women in Des Moines—and across Iowa—who were not only active in the suffrage movement but went on to promote informed citizenship for members of their communities. If this League disbanded, its members could have chosen to lend their talents to one or more of the numerous chapters of the Iowa Federation of Colored Women's Clubs (see Glossary Appendix), the Woman's Christian Temperance Union, or other organizations that matched their interests and pursued goals similar to the League's. The membership of the Iowa League and the Iowa Federation of Colored Women's Clubs shared similar characteristics and aims: well-educated and industrious female volunteers working for the betterment of their communities and state. Both groups operated in accordance with these principles: 1) "that every citizen's right to vote should be protected; 2) that every person should have access to free public education that provides equal opportunity for all; and 3) that no person or group should suffer legal, economic, or administrative discrimination." (2)

Like other early Leagues in Iowa, the Des Moines League of Colored Women Voters may have struggled with practicing the League principle of nonpartisanship, an issue that forced some Leagues in the state to disband during the first decade of their existence. The first Des Moines League and the first Davenport League both disbanded and were reinstated later when they embraced nonpartisanship. Just more than fifty years removed from slavery, African American communities in Iowa, as in the rest of the nation, generally continued to identify strongly with the Republicans—the party of Abraham Lincoln. Mrs. Brown was involved for several years in the National League of Republican Colored Women, so she may have chosen to concentrate her efforts in a partisan manner rather than through the League. Also, along with her work in the new Des Moines chapter of the National Association for the Advancement of Colored People, in the early 1920s she took on the time-consuming task of being grand matron of the Iowa Order of the Negro Eastern Star, a women's fraternal organization. Perhaps she chose not to lead the fledgling League of Colored Women Voters in order to focus her efforts on fighting for the rights of African Americans and women through her work in other organizations.

The Des Moines League of Colored Women Voters was one of only three Leagues of Colored Women Voters identified in archival searches, along with Fort Dodge and Keokuk. If the Des Moines organization did dissolve, members may have decided to join the League of Women Voters of Des Moines. Leagues in Iowa at that time were at least ostensibly open to any woman twenty-one or older. However, because the League has never collected race, ethnicity, or age data on members, and because records of local Leagues from the early years are difficult to find, membership statistics are impossible to document. The recent work of Carolyn Jefferson-Jenkins, the first woman of color to serve as president of the League of Women Voters of the United States (1994–98) and author of *The Untold Story of Women of Color in the League of Women Voters*, calls into question the League's acceptance of African American women during its early years. This would alter the previously presented interpretation of the demise of what may well have been the first local Iowa League. (See Chapter 12 for a glimpse at Dr. Jefferson-Jenkins's findings on the League's actions toward women of color from 1920 to the early 1970s.)

Former Iowa Leagues

Algona — Kossuth County

Atlantic — Cass County
LWVIA President: Kathryn Finkbine 1953–55

Baxter — Jasper County

Belmond — Wright County

Boone — Boone County

This city was the site of the 1908 suffrage parade. Soon after the League was established, League members conducted one of the first surveys of public utilities, a study that influenced future city decisions.

Burlington — Des Moines County
LWVIA President: Nellie Cray 1948–49

The Burlington chapter established community support networks for wives of Iowa Ordnance plant workers, at the USO's request, during World War II; recommended visiting teachers, help with court records, and a recreation center for juvenile delinquents, all of which were put in place; was one of just thirty U.S. cities included in a 1952 pre-convention forum titled "The Citizens' View of '52," aired by NBC Television; pushed for water fluoridation; and promoted the creation of the Des Moines County Health Center, the first one in Iowa. Notable members include Dorothy Schramm, a founder of this League in the late 1930s, who was renowned for her many talents and achievements. She was Iowa's first appointee to the National League Board in 1942; wrote the nationally recognized handbook "You are Democracy" in 1948; actively supported the United Nations (known as its "guiding force in Iowa"); combatted racism in the 1950s as a member and officer of the Iowa chapter of the NAACP; and was a 1986 inductee into the Iowa Women's Hall of Fame. Another League member, Margaret Raymond, was the first woman appointed to the Job Corps in the early 1960s.

Carroll — Carroll County

This League hosted James Schramm, husband of Burlington League leader Dorothy, for a 1962 community "Talk on Trade and Aid"; lobbied for a new courthouse in the 1960s, which was eventually built; and launched a Speakers' Bureau in 1968.

Clinton — Clinton County

Council Bluffs — Pottawattamie County

Estherville — Emmett County

The Estherville League may have been one of the first local Leagues formed in 1920 and began a Citizenship School in 1933.

Fairfield — Jefferson County

Fairfield Leaguers held panels on the United Nations and election laws.

Fort Dodge — Webster County

The *Bystander* reported that Fort Dodge women organized a League of Colored Women Voters in the early 1920s, though no other information has been found.

A quote from Claudine Navens in 1975: "Members are from all walks of life, and we make it clear we do not spend time discussing which cookie to serve; we concentrate on deeper subjects!"

Fort Madison — Des Moines County

Hamilton County

LWVIA Presidents: Janet Adams 1983–85 and Jan McNally 2001–03
Iowa Legislature: Janet Adams, House 1987–1993

The Hamilton County League studied the privatization of the county home in 1986 and provided precinct voter recorders for ABC Television that fall; designed and distributed a 1987 pamphlet titled "Lead in your Water"; conducted an adult daycare study in 1991 that resulted in the establishment of an adult daycare center; was one of ten local Leagues that in 1995 received a LWVUS grant for "Strengthening Women's Rights in the Newly Independent States," which funded three-week visits for one Russian and one Ukrainian representative to study local government and elections; hosted a 1998 Landfill Forum; and conducted a 2009 county fair straw poll on the bottle bill and five other issues before the Legislature, with a good response from fair attendees. In addition, as part of a national League initiative, member Mary Schultz and her husband Loren traveled to Bosnia to be election supervisors.

A quote from former LWVIA president and Iowa legislator Janet Adams, mother of seven: "Balancing family work and volunteer activities is a struggle at times but the benefits of gaining new information, meeting interesting new people, and bettering, changing, or eliminating a problem is worth the effort. I feel organization is an important skill for a woman with a family. Being a partner in a marriage and child rearing, as well as contributing financially, is rewarding and stressful. Women need to feel it is their right to pursue a career if they choose, but with the understanding that tradeoffs have to be made."

Humboldt — Humboldt County

This League may have been one of the first formed in 1920 under the name Bradgate.

Indianola — Warren County

Jane Wallerstedt founded the Indianola League; she later became an unpaid lobbyist for the League of Women Voters of Iowa before becoming a legislative aide.

Iowa Falls — Hardin County

Keokuk — Des Moines County

LWVIA President: Jean Meyer 1985–87

The *Daily Gate City and Constitution-Democrat*, a Keokuk newspaper, reported the formation on April 1, 1920, of a League of Colored Women Voters, with Mrs. Artesia Field Busch elected chairwoman and twice-monthly meetings planned.

Le Mars — Plymouth County

Marshalltown — Marshall County

The Marshalltown League may have been one of the first local Leagues formed in 1920. It could have stemmed from the previous presence of Carrie Lane Chapman in the community. She gave her first speech for suffrage in Marshalltown in 1887, when she and her husband owned a newspaper nearby.

Mason City/Clear Lake — Cerro Gordo County

LWVIA Presidents: Hazel Knutson 1926–28 and Mary Dresser Curtis 1965–69
Iowa Legislature: Betty J. Clark, House 1977–91

Clear Lake may have been another of the first local Leagues formed in 1920. Membership dues in 1947 were a dollar a year! This League placed a quarter-page ad in local newspapers to explain the differences between the manager plan and the mayor-council form of government in 1948 and sent flyers home with schoolchildren with the same information. After World War II, members educated the public about the United Nations with a series of workshops and studied the problems of people displaced by the war, a current issue in today's world. They studied school district reorganization and recreational facilities for the community, both accomplished in due time.

Monticello — Jones County

LWVIA President: Bernadine Smith 1941–43

The Monticello League, which also included Wyoming, Iowa, residents, was one of the original Leagues in the state. In 1933, members held a series of voters' schools and gave out carnations to voters at various elections in the county.

Mount Pleasant — Henry County

Mount Pleasant Leaguers sponsored instructional sessions for new voters in 1950; performed a skit for the community titled "New Congress Appropriations or Mamma Fights for Food" in 1953; held a public meeting to address the question "Is There a Place for Women on the Mt. Pleasant School Board?"; and between 1953 and 1956 studied waste disposal and sewers, and the city's street lights. League member Mrs. Eugene McCord headed the City Planning Commission in 1953.

Mount Vernon/Linn County
(Now a unit of Linn County League based in Cedar Rapids)

Iowa Legislature: Joan M. Lipsky, House 1967–79 and Joyce Lisbon Nielsen, House 1989–93

This League studied and acted upon water fluoridation in 1958 and soon after that supported a bond issue for a new city swimming pool; produced a local option sales tax information brochure in a joint venture with the Cedar Rapids-Marion League before a vote on the issue in 1986 and secured voters' support of the issue.

This League received the LWVIA Lee Kirkberg Memorial Action Award in 1991 for adopting and implementing a solid waste management program for the community; earned a second such award the next year for its study and action on the establishment of a school-aged childcare program across the street from an elementary school; and succeeded in 1993 in obtaining staggered terms for City Council members after many years of work.

Oelwein — Fayette County

Oskaloosa — Mahaska County, "A Tale of Two Leagues"

The Oskaloosa League formed in 1920 with Mary Anderson, head of the Women's Bureau of the U.S. Department of Labor, as its inaugural speaker. The early League operated primarily as a social organization. Monthly meetings devolved into luncheons featuring vocal selections and original poetry, not study and action of issues or discussion of voter registration activities. This group disbanded in 1925.

In 1955, Oskaloosa women formed a new League, this time with activities focused on League initiatives. In 1960, in collaboration with other community organizations, members held a public debate titled "Shall There Be a Convention to Revise the Iowa Constitution and Amend the Same?" featuring state Representative David Stanley of Muscatine arguing the affirmative and former state Senator Alan Vest arguing the negative.

In subsequent years, the League published a booklet in 1963 titled "Know Your County," which was used in social studies courses in junior and senior high schools and for several years by the Drake University Institute on State and Local Government. The League presented a "Politics in the Park" forum in 1976 as a venue for speeches by local candidates and a bicentennial celebration emphasizing the suffrage movement, with costumed suffragists, the reading of Abigail Adams's famous letter to husband John, and a re-enactment of a portion of the Seneca Falls Convention.

A partnership with the American Association of University Women in 1997 resulted in a Get Out the Vote Campaign using posters showing a woman with no mouth and captioned "Use your voice in the upcoming election!" In addition, the League in 1986 completed the Mahaska County Oral History Project to record and recognize the political and social contributions of Iowa women over the previous eighty-five years. Project organizers also sought to discern the economic influences on women's decision-making in terms of their personal and professional lives and to discover what support systems existed as avenues for women's creative, professional, and self-expression. Subjects for the project were Dora Wilson, 103; her daughter Myrtle Elwood, 83; Mary Louise Smith; and Louise Rosenfield Noun, 78, granddaughter of an Oskaloosa pioneer retailer who supplied early coal towns.

Pella — Marion County

The Pella League was founded in 1970. League members wrote and published "Myths about Housing—the Pella Story," "Sidewalks and Safety for the People of Pella," and biannual political directories. They also sponsored a radio show, probably to present and discuss issues such as traffic counts, senior citizen transportation, telephone service (those old kind of phones with an operator), lack of sufficient swimming pool hours, the need for bicycle paths and a community center, the impact of a proposed highway bypass, a needed emergency warning system, and a recycling program, all topics of study for this League.

In addition, members visited sites under study, including a coal strip mine, the city jail, the sewage treatment plant and water works, and the county dump. From Leaguer Elsie Maxim: "No one would go to the city dump alone; you just don't pick up and go there. The places that League members find exciting are not what everyone thinks is exciting; [we] find those kinds of places interesting and fun!" In 1997, this League successfully supported a bond issue for a new library.

This was the home League of longtime volunteer, *LWVIA Legislative Newsletter* reporter and volunteer lobbyist Joan Lucas. Along with comprehensive reporting to local Leagues on action during sessions of Iowa Legislature, she created Legistats, a subscription service for lobbyists, legislators, business owners, chamber of commerce members, and citizens that compiled a description of each bill, roll call votes by legislator, and a tabulation of the votes.

Perry — Dallas County

Scott County
(Also known as the Davenport League—Another "Tale of Two Leagues")

LWVIA Presidents: Harriet B. Chambers 1963–65 and Mona Martin 1981–83
Iowa Legislature: Mona Martin, House 1993–2001 and 2019 Iowa Women's Hall of Fame inductee; Maggie Tinsman, Senate 1989–2007 and 2014 Iowa Women's Hall of Fame inductee

Davenport's first League formed in 1920 but disbanded in 1938 when membership numbers dipped too low. The League reorganized in 1946 under the leadership of Lois Leach, mother of longtime Congressman Jim Leach. She later was an appointee to the national League Board of Directors in 1951. League members wrote and published a booklet titled "You are Democracy," which explained in a simple, detailed manner the workings of state and local government and the citizen's relationship to it. This booklet represented an ambitious effort to serve citizens. The League raised $6,000 to finance the project and gave a copy to every home in Scott County. Public schools found the booklet a valuable aid in civics and government classes for many years.

This League also was the first local League in Iowa to use the radio, station WOC, to broadcast information garnered from its studies and to encourage the public to become informed about upcoming decision-making at the city and county levels. The League also presented in 1968 the results of a Human Needs and Community Services of Scott County study and recommended a number of needed services related to health, family and children, employment and income maintenance, and recreation—fifty years ago, mind you—most of which came to fruition after a long period of advocacy.

In 1971, the League presented a study titled "Children in Trouble: A Survey of Programs and Services in Scott County." The next year, members requested a review by the Board of Supervisors of 1) the position of "overseer of the poor," and 2) the entire Scott County Department of Welfare—its goals, objectives, and outcomes. This League's position from its study was that the overseer position was unnecessary and that the department was not run efficiently and effectively. If the board did not act upon the League's concerns, the League requested a public referendum on each issue. At that point the board acted, eliminating the overseer position and making a plan for an improved welfare department. In 1985, the League conducted a study to improve and expand the biking and jogging trail system and establish an advisory commission for Davenport's Parks and Recreation Department. Both got done, of course!

Scott County LWV Bike Path Study Committee, September 1985. Pictured are Kay Whitmore, chair Mona Martin, Leslie Rasmus, Debbie Irey, Marcia Robertson, and two cooperative little riders.

Spencer — Clay County

Upper Iowa — Winneshiek County

This League was founded in Decorah in 2001 and held forums on local topics such as a county vote on underwriting an ethanol plant. The forums also addressed state and national League program issues, such as water quality, land use, Iowa's correctional system, health care, climate change, and clean elections. The League joined with the Iowa United Nations Association and Luther College on a global human rights forum and sponsored numerous community book discussion series. The group reluctantly disbanded in 2011 after a decade of work informing themselves and their community on important issues, ending with this statement: "You can't burn out if you're not on fire, and we were fired up for a decade!"

SPOTLIGHT ON LOCAL LEAGUES LWV of Mount Vernon-Lisbon

This fall, League perseverance prevailed in Mount Vernon. Twelve years ago a local League study and consequent consensus held that Mount Vernon City Council members should have staggered terms. Finally, it has happened.

For several elections voters failed to pass a referendum for staggered terms. Then in 1993, following an extensive League campaign, the local electorate passed it by a 3-1 margin. Last November the top vote-getters won longer terms. Staggered terms are now part of Mount Vernon city government. We are confident that this system will permit greater continuity, allow council more time to research public opinion before making decisions, and lead to a higher degree of competence among council members.

HATS OFF TO YOU ...

... Scott County for finding an innovative way to handle your files! Last spring the League of Women Voters of Scott County moved its files--both past and present--into the Davenport Public Library. Following up on an idea of a League member who had worked at the library but was now retired, the Board negotiated with the public library to house not only the archives of the League, but current files as well. The Scott County LWV agreed to assist in refiling according to library rules and, of course, all the files are open to the public as well as to the League.

PELLA'S OPERA HOUSE
by Dian Van Dalen
LWVIA Convention Co-Chair

Pella's newly restored opera house will provide a setting of grandeur for the 1991 annual Convention of the LWVIA on Saturday, April 13.

Newsletter clippings from former local Leagues: Mount Vernon — Lisbon, 1996 (top), Scott County "Hats Off to You," 1991 (above); Pella —Marion County "Pella's Opera House," 1991(left).

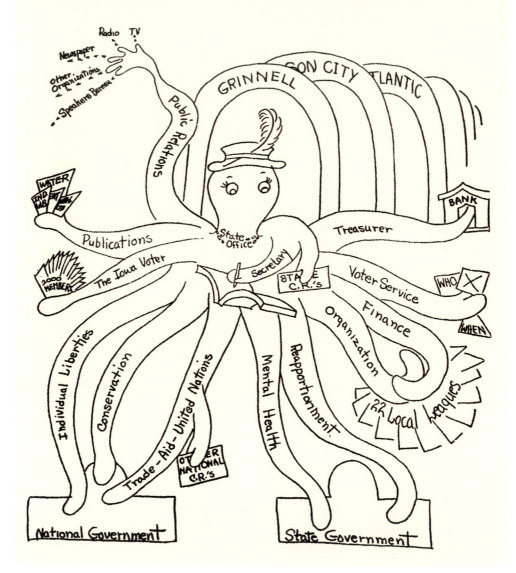

Artwork from the League of Women Voters of Iowa convention booklet, 1958.